BAKER STUDIES IN BIBLICAL ARCHAEOLOGY

TELL EL AMARNA
AND
THE BIBLE

BAKER STUDIES IN BIBLICAL ARCHAEOLOGY

TELL EL AMARNA
AND
THE BIBLE

by
Charles F. Pfeiffer

BAKER BOOK HOUSE
Grand Rapids, Michigan

Library of Congress Catalog Card Number: 62-20014

Copyright, 1963, by

Baker Book House Company

ISBN: 0-8010-7002-3

Third printing, December 1976

CONTENTS

Illustrations

PREFACE

The Amarna Age — the fifteenth and fourteenth centuries before Christ — provides the archaeologist rich resources for the study of ancient cultures. The epic and mythological literature from Ras Shamra, ancient Ugarit on the Phoenician coast, dates from this period, as do the Nuzi tablets written by Hurrian scribes in Mitanni. The Ugaritic texts give us an insight into the language and religious thought of ancient Canaan, and the archives from Nuzi offer a wealth of information concerning the social, economic, and legal structure of northern Mesopotamia in Patriarchal times.

During the Amarna Age the Hittite Empire was pushing southward from its center in Asia Minor, seeking to incorporate into its domains both independent states and areas that had acknowledged Egyptian sovereignty. Minoan Crete had already reached her highest achievements and was fast approaching her end. Babylon had already enjoyed a period of prosperity and power under the great Hammurabi, but she would not again become a major power for seven centuries — when Nebuchadnezzar would lead her to fresh victories. Assyria was soon to send her armies into Syria and Palestine and challenge Egypt for control of the East, but she was still a minor power during the Amarna Age.

The present study is limited to events in Egypt and to Egypt's political and military relations with her vassals in Syria and Palestine. The Amarna Tablets are our primary source of information for Egypt's external affairs, and the artifacts and tomb inscriptions from Amarna (ancient Akhetaton) help us to reconstruct life at the court of Akhenaton — the Pharaoh whose personality is apparent in every chapter.

The author expresses his indebtedness to the scholars whose books are listed in the bibliography, and to those organizations which made available the photographs which are an important part of the present study. The president and staff of the Baker Book House have shown every consideration in the planning of the series, Baker Studies in Biblical Archaeology, and in the production of this, the second volume.

Charles F. Pfeiffer

Central Michigan University
Mount Pleasant, Michigan

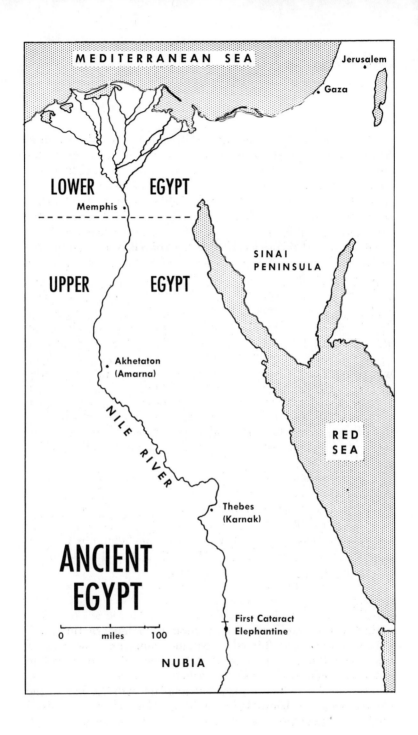

I

DISCOVERIES AT AMARNA

Early in the eighteenth century an Arab tribe known as the Beni Amran settled in a semicircular plain about one hundred ninety miles south of Cairo. Here, clustered along the east bank of the Nile, they built the villages of El Till, El Hag Quandil, El Amariah and Hawata. When the Danish traveler F. L. Norden visited the area in 1773 he noted that the natives called it Beni Amran, or Omarne. The name Tell el Amarna, by which it is popularly known today, seems to have been coined by John Gardner Wilkinson, the amateur Egyptologist who did so much to popularize Egyptian studies in Victorian Britain. Wilkinson combined the name of the village El Till (altered to the more common word *tell*, which means "mound" in Arabic) with the tribal name El Amarna, from the Beni Amran. The name Tell el Amarna is not strictly correct, for the ancient city of Akhetaton which occupied the site of Amarna does not have a succession of levels indicating different periods of occupation, such as archaeologists identify in the mounds of Palestine and Mesopotamia. Akhetaton was built to be the capital of Pharaoh Amenhotep IV, better known as Akhenaton, about 1365 B.C., and was abandoned half a century later.

The Beginnings

Egyptian archaeology gained impetus in modern times following Napoleon's ill-fated Egyptian campaign. The savants who accompanied the army of Napoleon studied Egyptian antiquities and discovered the trilingual inscription known as the Rosetta Stone which provided scholars with the key to the decipherment of hieroglyphic writing. That, in turn, enabled modern students to get a firsthand view of life in ancient Egypt,

instead of depending on references to Egypt in classical literature for basic information.

A French scholar, Jean Francois Champollion, studied the
Rosetta Stone in the light of his previous work in Coptic, a
late form of the Egyptian language which used a modified
Greek alphabet. After four years of research, in 1822 Champollion published his conclusions which provided a firm founda-
tion for the science of Egyptology which was soon added to the
curricula of the major universities of Europe. Scholars, both
professional and amateur, began making their way to Egypt to
copy inscriptions and study antiquities.

The rock tombs beyond the Amarna plain did not escape
these early travelers. During his explorations in Egypt from
1821 to 1831, John Gardner Wilkinson visited Amarna, and a
more systematic study of the nearby tombs was made by a
Prussian expedition directed by Karl Richard Lepsius from
1842 to 1845. Amarna art and inscriptions found a place in the
twelve volume work of Lepsius, *Denkmaler aus Aegypten und
Athiopien* (in English, *The Monuments from Egypt and Ethi-
opia*). The Prussians traced the ground plan of Akhetaton, ob-
serving the lines of its ancient streets. They noted that some of
the remains of the principal temple were still standing.

THE AMARNA TABLETS

It was late in 1887, however, before Amarna yielded its most
spectacular treasures, and even then it took some time before
their value was recognized. When mud brick walls decompose,
they form a nitrous soil which the Egyptians have learned to
use as fertilizer. A peasant woman, digging for this fertilizer
among the Amarna ruins, came upon a quantity of small baked
clay tablets bearing cuneiform inscriptions. Some of the tablets
were as small as two and one-eighth by one and eleven-sixteenths
inches, while others were as large as eight and three-quarters
by four and seven-eighth inches. Thousands of such tablets have
been found among the ruins of ancient Sumerian, Assyrian, and
Babylonian cities, where cuneiform was the normal means of
written communication from about 3000 B.C., when history
began, until the days of the Persian Empire (550-331 B.C.) when
Aramaic, using an alphabet script, took its place. Cuneiform,
however, seemed strangely out of place in Egypt. The woman
who had accidently come upon the tablets, not knowing their
value, is said to have disposed of her interest in the find

Amarna Tablets from the British Museum. The tablets comprise correspondence between the rulers of the nations and
city-states of western Asia and the Egyptian Pharaohs Amenhotep III and Amenhotep IV (Akhenaton).

for ten piasters — about fifty cents. The enterprising purchaser
knew that Europeans were paying for antiquities from Egypt
and he sought means of disposing of them at a good price.

An antiquities dealer showed wisdom in sending several of
the texts to a noted Assyriologist, Jules Oppert of Paris, doubtless thinking that Oppert might encourage the Louvre to pur-
chase them. Oppert had had extensive experience in archaeological work in the Near East. He had directed a French expedition at Babylon in 1852, and had subsequently been active
in the work of deciphering cuneiform inscriptions. When Jules
Oppert saw the Amarna tablets, however, he summarily dismissed them as forgeries. The story that they had been found
in Egypt may have been too much for him to take. Tablets
were also sent to the head of the Egyptian Department of
Antiquities, G. M. E. Grebaut, but he ventured no opinion concerning their worth. Perhaps he, too, was puzzled at the thought
of cuneiform inscriptions in Egypt.

Since the authorities had shown no interest in the tablets,
many of them were dumped into sacks and carried by donkey
to Luxor with the hope that dealers there might be able to

dispose of them through sale to tourists. In the process of transportation many of the tablets were literally ground to bits. Those that survived may be but a small fraction of the original archive.

Chauncey Murch, an American missionary stationed at Luxor, learned about the tablets and suspected they might be of real value. He, along with friendly antiquities dealers, brought them to the attention of E. A. Wallis Budge, Keeper of the Egyptian and Assyrian Antiquities in the British Museum, who happened to be in Egypt at the time for the purpose of adding to the museum collection. Budge was enthusiastic with what he saw, although he was by no means the only one who had come to realize that these little lumps of baked clay would be of inestimable value to the linguist and the historian of the ancient East. Although we have no way of knowing exactly how many of the tablets were irretrievably damaged or destroyed, about three hundred and fifty were preserved, and later discoveries increased the total number of Amarna tablets in the various collections to about four hundred.

Budge would have purchased the entire lot for the British Museum, but the tablets were in the hands of several dealers, some of whom had made agreements with an agent of the Berlin Museum for the sale of antiquities. As a result the British Museum and the Berlin Museum each acquired collections of Amarna Tablets, and smaller quantities went elsewhere. Budge acquired eighty-two for the British Museum and Theodore Graf of Vienna purchased about one hundred and eighty tablets which were sold to J. Simon of Berlin for presentation to the museum. The Berlin collection was subsequently increased to over two hundred. Sixty of the tablets remained in Cairo, twenty-two from a later discovery went to the Ashmolean Museum at Oxford, and the remainder are scattered among other museums and private collections. The Louvre has six, two are in the Metropolitan Museum in New York City, and one is in the Oriental Institute of the University of Chicago.

In 1892, Frederick J. Bliss, while excavating Tell el Hesi in southern Palestine discovered a cuneiform tablet which mentions a name known from the Amarna tablets. It evidently dates from the Amarna period. At Taanach, five miles southeast of Megiddo in northern Palestine, Ernst Sellin discovered four more letters in 1903. They date in the fifteenth century B.C., about three generations before the bulk of the Amarna tablets. As late as the winter of 1933-34, members of the Egyptian Exploration Society discovered eight additional tablets at the original site. Six of these were school texts and exercises used by students in the local academy where Egyptians were taught to read and write Akkadian.

Several of the Amarna tablets contain lists of signs and items of vocabulary. Others are practice copies of such Akkadian myths as *Adapa and the South Wind, Ereshkigal and Nergal,* and the *King of Battle* epic. Most, however, comprise the diplomatic correspondence of the Egyptian Foreign Office during the reigns of Amenhotep III and IV (Akhenaton). The archives included letters to and from Babylon (13 items), Assyria (2), Mitanni (13), Alashia (=Cyprus?) (8), the Hittites (at least 1). Two letters, written in a Hittite dialect, probably involve the king of Arzawa, a region along the southern coast of Asia Minor. One letter is written to the kings of Canaan demanding safe passage of a messenger who is on his way to Egypt. Another is a letter from a Babylonian princess to the Egyptian ruler. Most of the rest — actually about four-fifths of the whole collection — are letters to and from the rulers of city-states of Canaan (*Kinahni*), a name applying in general to Palestine, Syria, and Phoenicia; and the Amorites (*Amurru*) of Lebanon. This extensive correspondence enables us to reconstruct the political history of the Near East during the fifteenth and fourteenth centuries B.C., a period frequently called the Amarna Age. While neither the Egyptian Pharaohs nor the rulers of Canaanite city-states used Akkadian as their mother tongue, it served as the language of diplomacy among people with varied ethnic backgrounds.

EXCAVATIONS AT AMARNA

With the recognition of the nature and value of the Amarna texts, attention naturally turned to the place where they were discovered. In 1891 W. Flinders Petrie, who had already spent a decade in Egypt, began excavating the Amarna ruins. He cleared many of the official buildings in the center of the city, and several houses farther south. Near the village of El Till he discovered the painted pavements of Akhenaton's palace, and remains of the ornamental decorations of the palace itself. To the east of the palace was the chamber in which the Foreign Office records were kept. This was where the first Amarna Tablets were discovered in 1887, and here Petrie uncovered twenty-two additional fragments which comprise the collection now in the Ashmolean Museum.

From 1907 until the outbreak of World War I, a German expedition under the Deutsche Orient-Gesellschaft began the systematic excavation of the Amarna ruins. After several trial digs they undertook the excavation of the southern end of the site (1911), progressing northward along the ancient thoroughfare known as High Priest Street. The most impressive discovery of these years was the studio which belonged to the sculptor Thutmose, which contained some of the finest specimens of ancient Egyptian art. The famed painted limestone bust of Nofretete was the work of Thutmose. The studio also contained excellent heads of Akhenaton, and of the young princesses who graced the royal household.

The sculptures and rock tombs, first described by Wilkinson and Lepsius, were subjected to vandalism by peasants who found that they could make money by chipping off sections of the inscriptions and selling them as antiquities. Fortunately this was halted by action of the Egyptian government, and a definitive study of the tombs was made by the Mission Archeologique Francaise and the Egypt Exploration Fund. The results were published in a definitive six volume work, *The Rock Tombs of El Amarna* by N. deGaris Davies from 1903 to 1908.

Since World War I, archeological work at Amarna has been the responsibility of the Egypt Exploration Society. T. Eric Peet and Leonard Woolley conducted a series of campaigns beginning in 1921 during which they continued the work of the Germans at the southern section of the town. They excavated the pleasure palace known as Meru Aton and much of the walled village inhabited by the ancient workmen who labored in the rock tombs east of the city. Tomb chapels were excavated north of the workmen's village, and a sanctuary known as the River Temple was discovered in the village of El Hag Qandil.

During the 1923-24 campaign, F. G. Newton and F. Llewellyn Griffith continued work in the southern sector and began excavation of the North Palace, north of El Till. The following season, following Newton's death, Thomas Whittemore completed work at the North Palace and adjacent structures. From 1926 to 1929 the work was directed by Henri Frankfort who continued excavating in the north and gave particular attention to work in the neighborhood of the Great Temple. John D. S. Pendlebury, who took over direction of the work in 1930, completed excavations in the north. In a series of campaigns between 1931 and 1937, Pendlebury directed work on the official quarters of the central city, including the palace and the Great Temple.

Archaeological work was concluded at Amarna in 1937. The site had great advantages, for it was the one city of Egypt which was never rebuilt. Most of our knowledge of ancient Egypt comes from discoveries in desert tombs, for ancient cities were usually replaced by modern cities on the same site. Akhetaton, however, was the sacred city of a Pharaoh whom later generations despised as a criminal; and after his death its significance was at an end. Just because it was not rebuilt centuries ago, today it yields an impressive picture of the times of Akhenaton.

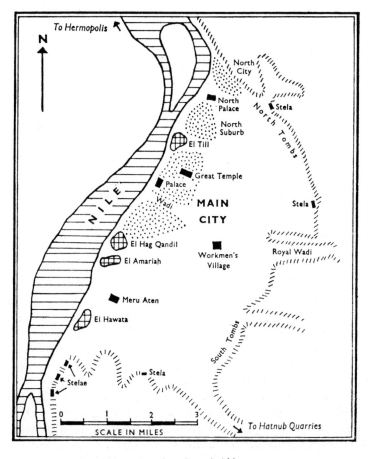

Akhetaton, the city of Akhenaton.

II

THE RESTLESS PHARAOH

Although Pharaohs of the third millenium B.C. exploited Sinai copper mines, and Middle Kingdom rulers sent trading expeditions to Punt on the African coast, opposite Aden, Egypt alone was considered to be a civilized land and foreigners could be dismissed as uncouth barbarians. Egypt lived in splendid isolation, annoyed at times by Semites who had infiltrated the fertile Nile Valley since prehistoric times, but never seriously involved in life beyond her borders. Her land appeared to be particularly favored of the gods, and the Egyptian could not think of it otherwise.

Yet the blessings of life along the Nile did not insure to Egypt a government that could meet challenges from without and guarantee peace and prosperity within the Nile Valley and Delta. By about 1700 B.C., Egypt experienced the weakening of central authority which permitted the invading Hyksos ("rulers of foreign lands") to seize control of the country and establish their own dynasty. The prosperous Middle Kingdom was at an end, and the hard hand of alien rule was evident throughout the land. It was not until 1570 B.C. that Ahmose, founder of the Eighteenth Dynasty, succeeded in driving the Hyksos back into Asia and establishing native control over Egypt.

THE NEW KINGDOM

The Hyksos invasion left one lesson: Never again could Egypt adopt a policy of isolation. The best defense is offense. As Asiatic Hyksos rulers had marched upon Egypt, so Egypt would march her armies into Asia. Thutmose I (1525-1494 B.C.) campaigned successfully in Asia, and under Thutmose III (1490-1435 B.C.) western Asia was brought under the control of

16

Egyptian arms. During his seventeen campaigns in Palestine and Syria, Thutmose III took Megiddo in the Valley of Esdraelon and Carchemish on the Euphrates. Egyptian authority extended from the Sudan to the Euphrates, and the reigning Pharaoh was suzerain of Syria and Palestine. The king list at Karnak lists one hundred nineteen towns taken by Thutmose III. Often the Egyptians were content to allow a native prince to remain in power as long as he was willing to provide tribute and manpower to the Egyptian commissioner. Important cities were ruled directly by an Egyptian governor.

In theory the Pharaoh was a god with absolute power whose word was law. The Egyptians have left us no law codes, and it may be that they sensed no need of such codified law as we find in Sumer, Babylon, Assyria, and among the Hittites (as well as the Biblical Hebrews). The presence of a living god in the land might render such written codes unnecessary.

In practice, however, as Egypt extended her Empire the personal involvment of the Pharaoh became progressively less. The priesthood of Amon-Re, god of Thebes and chief god of the Egyptian pantheon, developed enormous power. Before any important decision it was expected that the Pharaoh would consult the oracle of Amon-Re. Hundreds of civil servants were required to care for the needs of a great Empire, and most of these were drawn from a few powerful families. The result was a bureaucracy which, like the priesthood, could serve as a power block. The army, and particularly its commander, was a third factor that could not be ignored by Egyptian officialdom. While the Pharaoh was theoretically the head of church and state — god and king in Egypt — in practice he might find himself frustrated at every turn by religious, civil, and military bureaucracies.

From the campaigns of Thutmose III until late in the reign of Amenhotep III (ca. 1360 B.C.) the Egyptian Empire seems to have functioned with maximum efficiency. The riches of Nubia, Crete, western Asia, and even distant Mycene poured into Thebes, the Egyptian capital. A Mitannian princess graced the harem of Thutmose IV (1414-1406 B.C.). Amenhotep III caused his name and that of his wife to be cut into a group of scarabs with the inscription, "She is the wife of the victorious king whose territory in the south reaches to Karei (= Napata, at the Fourth Cataract of the Nile) and on the north to Naharin (=Mitanni)."[1]

---

1 Alan Gardiner, *Egypt of the Pharaohs* (Oxford: 1961), p. 207

Commemorative Scarab of Amenhotep III.
Issued on the occasion of the construction
of a pleasure lake for Queen Tiy: (above)
side view, and (right) inscription.

Amenhotep III. The brown
quartzite head depicts the Pharaoh with an enigmatic smile.

Amenhotep III was responsible for the immense colonnades at Luxor and a great funerary temple which has disappeared except for two immense seated statues of the Pharaoh now known as the Colossi of Memmon (supposedly representing an Ethiopian hero who fell on the battlefield at Troy). Although the harem of Amenhotep III included daughters from the kings of Mitanni, Assyria, Babylon, and the Hittites, he was devoted to his wife Tiy for whom he built an artificial lake a mile long and over a thousand feet wide south of the Medinet Habu temple.

The decline in Egyptian power may be traced to the latter half of the reign of Amenhotep III. While the Pharaoh was sick, his wife Tiy seems to have exercised considerable power. The balance of power in Asia was upset by the rise of Suppiluliumas (1375-1340 B.C.), a Hittite ruler who sought to carve out an empire for himself. Egypt avoided military action, with the result that the loyal princes were left to defend themselves or make their own terms with the enemy.

Young Amenhotep IV

When Amenhotep III died he was succeeded by his eleven year old son Amenhotep IV (1370-1353 B.C.), and the queen mother Tiy continued to act as regent. In addition to the influence of his mother, young Amenhotep IV was educated by the priest, Eye, who was the husband of his childhood nurse. No doubt Amenhotep was early married to the fair Nofretete who may have been his sister. Brother-sister marriages were common in ancient Egypt, but we cannot be certain concerning the parentage of Nofretete. Under the tutelage of his mother, his wife, and a favored priest, young Amenhotep could hardly be expected to have developed an interest in military affairs. His interest turned toward religion and, in the words of Breasted, "the philosophizing theology of the priests was of more importance to him than all the provinces of Asia."[2]

Amenhotep IV is depicted as having a thin face, narrow sloping shoulders, and unusually large hips and abdomen. His skull seems to have been deformed, and he may have been an epileptic. These handicaps did not affect his mind, however, for he was one of history's creative thinkers. Breasted (with considerable hyperbole, to be sure), calls him "the first individual in

---

2 James Breasted, A History of Egypt (New York: 1909), p. 356

human history."[3] Unfortunately the international tensions of the day were such that Egypt needed a warrior rather than a philosopher king. The idealism of Amenhotep IV was largely lost on his own generation, and entirely lost on the generation that followed him.

Nofretete was devoted both to her husband and to the religious reforms to which he dedicated his life. She bore him six daughters and appears to have been her husband's constant companion and confidant. Nofretete was, understandably, a favored subject in Amarna art. Reliefs depict her playing with her daughters, and one shows her seated on her husband's knee, blowing him a kiss at a chariot procession.

During the early years of his reign, Amenhotep IV clearly favored the god Aton, but he was tolerant of the various deities worshiped in Egypt. In this he continued the policy of his father, Amenhotep III, and his mother, Queen Tiy. The preference for the god Aton is evident in the name of the first child of Amenhotep IV, Merit-aton ("Beloved of Aton").

The priests of Amon in Thebes must have looked with apprehension upon the youthful Pharaoh whose devotion to the chief god of Egypt seemed to be compromised by religious innovation. We can only guess their reaction when Amenhotep IV decided to build a temple to Aton within the sacred precincts of the city of Amon. Orders were given to quarry sandstone at the Silsila quarries, forty miles north of Aswan. Here a monument was erected to mark the beginning of the quarrying operation:

> First occurrence of His Majesty's giving command to muster all the workmen from Elephantine to Samhudet, and the leaders of the army, in order to make a great breach for cutting out sandstone, in order to make the sanctuary of Harakhti in his name, "Heat which is in Aton," in Karnak. Behold the officials, the companions, and the chiefs of the fan bearers were the chiefs of the quarry service for the transportation of stone.[4]

Amenhotep IV was twenty-one when he created the Aton temple at Thebes. He was still attempting to form a synthesis of old and new elements in his religious faith, for the old god Re-Harakhti of Heliopolis is identified with Aton. The Silsila stele depicts Amenhotep IV worshiping Amon, yet it also shows Aton (the sun) with rays of light which hold the Egyptian sign of life (*ankh*). Amon, Re-Harakhti, and Aton all figure in the Silsila stele.

---

3 *Ibid.*
4 James H. Breasted, Ancient Records of Egypt, II (Chicago: 1906), p. 935

Akhenaton and Nofretete. A limestone
plaque from Akhetaton depicts the Pharaoh
and his beautiful wife.

THE BREAK WITH AMON

Amenhotep IV, however, was unable to stop with half-way
measures. In his devotion to Aton he felt that his god alone was
worthy of worship. The Theban temple area was renamed, "The
Brightness of the Great Aton," and the city itself became, "The
City of the Brightness of Aton." In an obvious break with the
past, Amenhotep IV determined to change his own name, which
meant "Amon is satisfied" to Akhenaton, meaning, "he who is
serviceable to Aton."

From this time on, Akhenaton's zeal knew no bounds. He
banished the mention of Re-Harakhti from the descriptive title
of Aton, and had the very names of Amon and the Egyptian
pantheon chiseled out of the monuments at Thebes. The Amon
temples were closed, and Atonism became the only sanctioned
religion of Egypt. The reform, however, did not have a popular
base, and it probably did not penetrate far beyond the royal
family and retainers. Akhenaton, like the earlier Pharaohs, be-

lieved in his own divinity, esteeming himself the son of Aton. As such he would be worshiped by his faithful subjects.

The reasons for Akhenaton's break with the religious traditions of his day are complex. In part the revolt certainly represents the desire of a young Pharaoh to free himself from the yoke of a firmly entrenched priestly class. Yet the break was far more than an act of political expediency. The influence of the priesthood of Heliopolis, perennial rivals of the Theban priests, and the development of Atonism in the years preceding his accession to the throne are all factors that cannot be overlooked. Perhaps the "petticoat government" into which he moved at the age of eleven with the strong influence of his mother, Queen Tiy, had something to do with it. There may even be a measure of com-

Seated Figure of Akhenaton. (at left) The young king is depicted in a conventional pose at Thebes before he moved his capital to Akhetaton. (at right—detail) The young Akhenaton is presented with a crook and flail in his hand, symbolizing authority, and the uraeus, symbol of royalty, at his head. The uraeus is a stylized representation of an enraged female cobra, poised as though prepared to strike an enemy.

pensation for physical inadequacies in the vigorous measures he took to establish Aton as the sole god of Egypt. Whatever historical or psychological motivations may be suggested, Akhenaton's whole life gives evidence of the fact that he was piously devoted to Aton, the god whose beneficent rays bring life to all mankind.

While the priests of Amon were bitterly antagonistic to Akhenaton, he found allies in the priests from Memphis who had long resented the dominating position of the Theban priesthood. The army was divided. Conservative elements sided with the Theban priests, but a bright young general, Horemhab, saw in Akhenaton's revolt an opportunity for personal advancement and threw in his lot with the new king. There is a suggestion that a counter revolution was planned, for the Amon priests claimed that the Pharaoh had abandoned his people, and was himself abandoned by his father Amon.

The New Capital

Akhenaton did abandon Thebes. As tensions grew he came to realize that his new faith could not flourish in the city of Amon. There were theological reasons, too, for Aton had no city that was distinctly dedicated to his worship. Akhenaton decided to build a new capital, dedicated to the god Aton, with the name Akhetaton, "the horizon of Aton."

The move to Akhetaton, modern Amarna, three hundred miles north of Thebes, must have been welcome both to Akhenaton's court and the Theban priesthood. The city seems to have been built in haste, and when Akhenaton left Thebes it was for good. Was life at Akhetaton all that Akhenaton envisioned? The inscriptions and the paintings from the rock tombs suggest that the royal family enjoyed a few happy years in devotion to Aton and to one another. True, the envoys from distant lands and subject peoples noted the growing gulf between Akhenaton and the people, and the empire suffered as the Egyptian Pharaoh lived in the seclusion of his capital. Tragedy entered the lives of Akhenaton and Nofretete when their second daughter Meketaton died and was buried in the family tomb east of Akhetaton.

The End of an Era

The closing years of the lives of Nofretete and Akhenaton are largely a blank. Their third daughter Meritaton married Smenkhkare, a young architect who was much favored by Akhenaton

A Princess at Akhetaton. A limestone relief showing one of the daughters of Akhenaton and his wife Nofretete discovered at Amarna.

Princess Manyet-aton. A representation of the princess was adapted for use as the lid of a canopic jar used in the burial of Akhenaton. Discovered in the tomb of Smenkhkare in the Valley of the Kings, Thebes.

and occupied the throne for a short time after his death. Another daughter Ankhsenpaton, married Tutankhaton, a loyal follower of her father. His brief reign left no impress on Egyptian history. The discovery of his tomb, however, in the Valley of the Kings, has made him the best known of all Pharaohs.

The circumstances concerning the deaths of Nofretete and Akhenaton are not known, although we do know that Akhenaton died in the seventeenth year of his reign, when he was but thirty years of age. Atonism did not long survive its most loyal adherents. Meritaton became Meritamon, and the famed King Tut is known by his later name, Tutankhamon, rather than the earlier Tuntankhaton. In many ways Akhenaton seems to have been a man whose life was a failure. All for which he stood was quickly obliterated during the scant generation after his death. Yet this judgment is too hasty. Even the priests of Amon could not wholly turn back the reforms in art and literature which Akhenaton encouraged. While such terms as "monotheist" and "pacifist" when applied to him bear a different connotation from their meaning in contemporary life, still his meditation upon the Aton bringing blessing to all men has within it the seed of

something that finds its highest expression in the prophetic
spokesmen of ancient Israel. Akhenaton went too far for his
own generation in Egypt, but the Biblical affirmation of God
as creator of heaven and earth and redeemer of mankind was
hardly apprehended by Akhenaton.

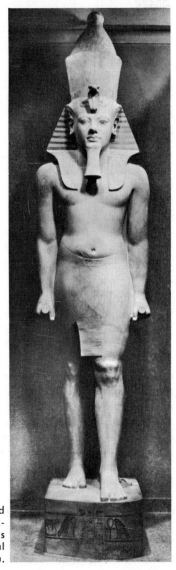

King Tutankhamon. Under the famed
"King Tut" the religious reforms of Akhenaton were renounced and Amon was
restored to his place as the principal
god of Egypt. Statue from Medinet Habu.

III

THE HORIZON OF ATON

When Akhenaton determined to build a new city which would be sacred to his god Aton, he chose a site on the east bank of the Nile, three hundred miles north of Thebes, where the flanking cliffs recede to leave a semicircular plain eight miles long and three broad. Here Akhenaton built the capital city which he named Akhetaton, "the horizon of Aton." The city itself was five miles long but only about eleven hundred yards broad. It had no walls, for the Nile formed its western boundary and a semicircle of cliffs bound it on the east. The fertile land along the river bank was kept for cultivation.

The Boundaries of Akhetaton

Akhenaton and his wife Nofretete personally chose the site of Akhetaton and supervised the erection of the stelae which marked its boundaries. In all, fourteen of these markers have been found on the hillsides east and west of the Nile. They contain a longer and a shorter version of the ceremony by which the site was consecrated. The shorter version tells how, on the eighth month of the sixth year of Akhenaton's reign, he mounted his golden chariot and journeyed northward from the richly ornamented tent where he had passed the night to fix the limits of the projected city of Akhetaton. After sacrificing to his god, Aton, he drove southward to a spot where the rays of the sun shining on him indicated where the southern boundary should be located. Here he swore an oath by his father Aton, and by his hope that the queen and his two (elder) daughters would attain old age, that he would never pass beyond this boundary, and beyond two more on the east bank and three on the west bank. All land within that area belonged to Aton, and should any damage befall the stelae marking it, he would make it good. Mention is made of a renewal of the oath in the eighth year.

The longer version adds some details. It tells how Akhenaton called his courtiers and military commanders, explaining to them Aton's wish that Akhetaton be built. Aton alone knew the site, and it is his alone. The courtiers reply that all countries will send gifts to Aton. Akhenaton praises his god and vows that he will never extend the citiy's boundaries, nor allow his wife to persuade him to do so. Then he enumerates the sanctuaries he will build at Akhetaton, ending with a reference to his family tomb.[1]

The pledge never to extend the boundaries of Akhetaton is puzzling. It seems to be a concession to the Amon priesthood that he will limit Aton's holdings to the few miles of territory in the region of present day Amarna. On the other hand the pledge may be merely the legal phrase used by a property owner to indicate that he has no rights beyond his own boundaries.

The Move to the New Capital

It probably took at least two years to build Akhetaton. It was during the sixth year of Akhenaton's reign that he ordered all Egyptians and subject peoples — Nubians and Asiatics — to serve Aton alone. Statues of the old gods were ordered destroyed; their reliefs were to be erased, and their names blotted out. Two years later — Akhenaton's eighth — the transfer of the capital from Thebes to Akhetaton was complete.

There are evidences of great haste in the construction of the buildings. Often naturalistic pictures of birds and vegetation painted on plaster walls and floors cover shoddy workmanship. Houses were built of mud brick, but palaces and temples were built of stone. An inscription attributed to the architect Bek at Aswan states that stone was quarried there "for the great and mighty monuments of the king in the house of Aton in Akhetaton."

The Plan of the City

Paralleling the Nile, the city had three north-south streets which crossed the more numerous east-west streets at right angles. The principal north-south street, the King's Way, served the city's more important buildings. At its southern end was the pleasure palace, Meru Aton, with its artificial pools, flower

---

1 Texts in N. deG. Davies, *The Rock Tombs of El Amarna*, V (London: 1908)

beds, and groves of trees. Meru Aton is thought to have served as a summer palace. It had a reception hall, a small chamber, guard houses, and various other buildings. The inner rooms were gaily decorated with colored columns and pavements painted with flying birds, playing animals, and a variety of plant life.

Farther north the King's Way passed between the palace and the royal house, where it was spanned by a bridge. In the center of the bridge was the "window of appearing" where the royal family appeared on special occasions to greet the populace assembled on the street below. The palace was fourteen hundred feet long and four to five hundred feet wide, with an impressive hall of pillars. The pavements of painted stucco, discovered by Flinders Petrie during his expedition at Amarna in 1891, were maliciously destroyed by a disgruntled guard in 1912, and the portions that were salvaged are now in the Cairo Museum. The royal house was a vast walled compound containing the king's apartment, a nursery for the princesses, and vast gardens and storehouses. The rooms were ornamented with colorful paintings and inlays of colored stone.

Beyond the palace, the King's Way passed the spiritual center of the royal city, the Great Temple to Aton, comprising a series of open courts and halls, connected by pylons in which altars were set up to receive offerings. The chief altar was located in the center of the largest court. Here Akhenaton, usually accompanied by Nofretete, offered prayers and consecrated offerings to Aton. Throughout the city there were numerous smaller shrines built to honor the kings of Egypt's past, or to serve members of the royal family. Nofretete presided at a shrine with the colorful name, "The House of Putting the Aton to Rest." The queen mother Tiy had a temple, and there were shrines for Baktaton, the king's younger sister, and Meritaton, his oldest daughter. Shrines were built in memory of Amenhotep II and Thutmose IV.

Beyond the Great Temple, the King's Way becomes the main street of modern El Till. It disappears for a time in the fields, but emerges at the North Palace which had walls decorated with lively paintings of bird life in a papyrus swamp. A royal aviary and a zoo were part of the palace complex. After another break, the lines of the ancient King's Way appear again in the northern city with its numerous mansions.

A second important north-south thoroughfare is High Priest Street from which the estates of many of the nobles in Akhenaton's court could be entered. The standard of living was one of luxury, for the houses of the nobles contained large reception halls, living rooms, and bedrooms. Each had a well-kept garden, at one end of which an avenue of trees led to a pool. Besides the spacious living quarters there were separate buildings to serve as stables for the flocks and herds belonging to the family, storage buildings, and servant's quarters. The largest such estate, belonging to the vizier Nakht, measured ninety-five by eighty-five feet.

Interspersed among these palatial homes were humbler cottages, belonging to the working class, each of which had a front hall, a living room, bedroom, and kitchen. Every house — both of nobles and of commoners — had a bathroom with running water and a lavatory. There was evidently no conscious city planning, for it seems that the nobles laid claim to extensive patches of land, only to surrender parts of their property to commoners at a later time. Perhaps unintentionally, Akhetaton has marks of democracy in this mixture of ruling and working classes.

The officials of Akhetaton were for the most part new appointments of the king, and many seem to have been chosen from among commoners who were sympathetic with Akhenaton's

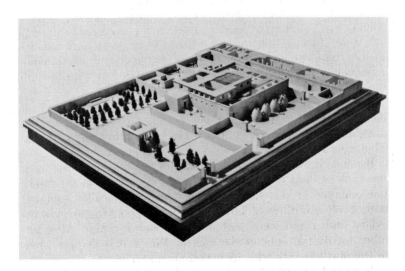

The Estate of a Nobleman. The model of the estate of one of Akhenaton's nobles at Akhetaton. Restoration by Seton Lloyd.

program. The mayor of the city bore the revealing name, "Akhenaton created me." Other officials include a captain of police,
an overseer of the treasury, the king's standard bearer, the commander of the army, overseers of the royal harem, the chief
physician, and priests of the various temples. Eye, who had been
a counselor of Akhenaton from boyhood, bore the impressive
title, "Superintendent of the King's Horses," implying a responsibility for the chariots of the royal army. Second only to Akhenaton himself was the vizier, a man named Nakht. A royal butler,
Parennufe, was one of the few officials who had served Akhenaton earlier in Thebes.

The Rock Tombs

The third north-south street was the East Road, located nearest to the desert and the rock tombs. As the earlier Pharaohs in
Thebes prepared tombs for themselves in the nearby Valley of
the Kings, so Akhenaton and his courtiers cut rock tombs into
the hillside east of Akhetaton. There are twenty-five of these
tombs with decorated walls honoring Aton and his son, Akhenaton. Davies in his *Rock Tombs of El Amarna* says,

> The scenes in the tombs of El-'Amarna, though abundant and
> detailed, yield us very limited information concerning men and
> things in Akhetaten. Taken together, they only reveal one per-
> sonality, one family, one home, one career, and one mode of
> worship. This is the figure, family, palace and occupations of
> the king, and the worship of the sun — which also was his, and
> perhaps, in strictness, of no one else. Into whatever tomb we
> enter, as soon as the threshold is past we might fancy ourselves
> in the royal sepulchre. The king's figure, family, and retinue
> dominate everything. It is his wife and children, his family
> affection, his house and treasures which are here portrayed in
> detail, and it is with difficulty sometimes that we discover among
> the crowd of courtiers the official whose tomb it is, distinguished
> by a little hieroglyphic label.[2]

The family tomb which Akhenaton built in the eastern desert,
four miles from the city, was used for the burial of his daughter,
the princess Meketaton. Most of the rock tombs, however, were
never occupied. Within a short time of the death of Akhenaton,
his capital was abandoned and Thebes again became the
center of government. Everything of value was removed from
Akhetaton — even the wooden pillars of the houses! The very
stones of the Aton temple were dragged away to be used in the
reconstruction of temples desecrated in the days of Akhenaton's
reform movement. Thus the priests of Amon had their revenge.

---

2 Vol. I (London: 1903), p. 19

IV

ATONISM

Akhenaton thought of himself as the apostle of Atonism, and he exhibited a mystical devotion to his god. Yet Akhenaton was not the founder of the Aton cult, which may be traced to antecedents in Egypt's earliest religious traditions.[1] The Sinuhe story, recounting the death of Amenemhet I (*ca.* 1960 B.C.), states that the deceased Pharaoh ascended to heaven and was united to the disk of the sun *(itn)*. While this may mean only that the sun disk was the abode of deity, it suggests the possibility that the Aton (sun disk) might itself become an object of worship.

ANCIENT EGYPTIAN RELIGION

The Egyptian religion of historical times represents a fusion of previously independent local gods. Each town was devoted to a particular deity, many of whom were represented in the form of animals. The cat goddess Bast was honored at Bubastis; the cobra-headed Edjo, at Buto; the ibis Thoth, at Hermopolis Magna; and the jackal god Wepwawet, at Lycopolis. Animal deities were frequently given the bodies and limbs of humans.

The sun and the Nile River were the two important factors in the life of all Egyptians, and gods associated with these phenomena tended to transcend Egyptian provincialism and become truly national in scope. The priests at Heliopolis, near ancient Memphis, were devoted to the worship of the sun god under his ancient name Re. Heliopolis ("city of the sun") is the Greek form of a name that appears in the Old Testament in translitera-

---

1 The originality of Akhenaton's contribution to Egyptian life is challenged by L. A. White, "Ikhanton; the Great *vs.* the Culture Process," *Journal of the American Oriental Society,* LXVIII (1948), pp. 91-114. He is answered by W. F. Edgerton, "The Great Man: A note on methods." *Ibid.* pp. 192-193

tion from the Egyptian as On (cf. Gen. 41:45ff.) and as Hebrew, Beth-Shemesh, "House of the sun" (Jer. 43:13). Joseph was married to an Egyptian girl named Asenath, "she belongs to (the goddess) Neith," the daughter of a priest named Potiphera ("He whom Re has given") who ministered at the shrine to the sun god at On, or Heliopolis (Gen. 41:45, 50; 46:20).

Re as the sun god came to be associated with other deities. As Re-Atum he came to be regarded as a manifestation of Atum, the creator. As god of the horizon, Re took the compound name Re-Harakhti. Such compounds as Sobek-Re and Khnum-Re indicate the tendency to identify local deities with the more universal Re. Beginning with the Fifth Dynasty (*ca.* 2500 B.C.) each Pharaoh bore the title "Son of Re" as part of his name, further enhancing the name and reputation of the sun god. Until the Egyptian New Kingdom (*ca.* 1600-1100 B.C.), when Amon of Thebes became the principal god of Egypt, the priests of Re at Heliopolis shared with the priests of Ptah in nearby Memphis the position of highest influence and wealth in the religious life of the country.

As creator god, Re was symbolized by the falcon and the scarab. The sun's daily journey across the sky reminded the de-

Hapi, God of the Nile. The Nile god is depicted on a relief from the throne of the Pharaoh Eye.

vout Egyptian of Re's first appearance as the originator of life.
Re, himself, was self-created according to the Book of the Dead.
In Middle Kingdom times (*ca.* 2000-1600 B.C.), Thebes became
the Egyptian capital and its patron deity Amon was identified
with the sun god and assumed the compound name "Amon-Re,
king of the gods." Thus a purely local god, through identification with Re, became the national god. As local gods became
identified with one another, or with more universal gods, we
may observe a tendency in the direction of monotheism.

Aton Worship

The worship of Aton appears as early as the reign of Thutmose
IV (*ca.* 1414-1406 B.C.), who issued a commemorative scarab
stating that the Pharaoh fought "with the Aton before him," and
that he campaigned abroad, "to make the foreigners to be like
the (Egyptian) people, in order to serve the Aton forever."[2]
Aton occupied an important place in the Egyptian pantheon
during the reign of Akhenaton's father, Amenhotep III. A stele of
the king's architects, Hori and Suti, describes the sun god as
the deity who holds sway over all peoples and lands. A hymn
speaks of Amon as "Aton of the day, creator of mortals and
maker of life." The royal barge of Amenhotep III and his wife
Tiy bore the name, "Aton gleams." Other gods were worshiped,
and Amon was still in his place of honor, but Aton had come to
the fore — perhaps in a context of rivalry between the priests of
Heliopolis and Thebes — and the stage was set for the impend-
ing battle.

In the earliest period of Akhenaton's reign, Aton was the pre-
ferred god, but Amon was still granted homage. There was
actually little that was original in the religious life of those
earliest years, although there was much that might give concern
to the Amon priests. Although there had been an earlier Aton
temple in Thebes, it was Akhenaton who slowly moved from a
position in which Aton was the favored god to one in which
Aton was the only god tolerated. While there had been tendencies toward monotheism before, and Aton worship was not new,
it was Akhenaton who finally made the break with the Amon
priests at Thebes. With inexorable logic he changed his name
from Amenhotep to Akhenaton, closed the Amon temples, and
erased the name of Amon from monuments and inscriptions.

---

2 A. W. Shorter, "Historical Scarabs of Tuthmosis IV and Amenophis III," *Journal
of Egyptian Archaeology,* XVII (1931), pp. 23-25. See also XVIII (1932), pp. 110-111;
XXII (1936) pp. 3-7

While Amon was the particular object of his disfavor, Akhenaton declared war on all the "thousand gods of Egypt," and sought to remove the very word "gods" from the monuments.

THE TRIUMPH OF ATON

Aton became the only object of worship tolerated by the Pharaoh, and his domain was extended beyond the boundaries of Egypt. Not only was the Egyptian capital moved to a city dedicated to Aton, but other cities were dedicated to him in Nubia and in Asia. The *Hymn to the Aton* expresses the same type of universalism, envisioning Aton (the sun) as the god who blesses all people everywhere. While the Nile might have served as a god to unite all Egyptians, the sun was a deity who might unite all men in a common brotherhood. This, at any rate, seems to have been Akhenaton's dream.

There remained, however, illogical elements in the monotheism of Akhenaton. The Pharaoh himself was still a god, and Akhenaton had no doubt that he was the divine son of Aton. While Akhenaton and the royal family paid homage to Aton, others stood in awe before the Pharaoh. There were elements in the Amarna faith which militated against this, particularly the realism which enabled the citizens of Akhetaton to caricature their king, but the concept of a divine Pharaoh persisted in the Aton cult.

No image represented Aton in human shape, as the "thousand gods" of Egypt had been represented. Instead, worship was directed toward the disk of the sun which exerts a life-giving influence through its rays which produce a brilliance and warmth that no man can fail to experience. The symbol of the god Aton was a solar disk from which rays of light descended, terminating in human hands, some of which hold the Egyptian sign of life *(ankh)*. In this symbolism, the sun graciously bestows life upon the worshiper of Aton. Sometimes the royal uraeus, symbol of kingship, hangs from the sun disk, and often it rises from the bottom of the disk toward the center. Aton is thus depicted as ruler as well as deity of all upon whom he shines.

While the Aton temple was not basically different from other shrines of ancient Egypt, it boasted no image and conducted its most solemn rites in the open, under the direct rays of the sun. This formed a distinct contrast to the cult of Amon who was called "the hidden one," and who had his shrine in the innermost and darkest part of the temple. If Amonism stressed the

The Beneficent Aton. The sun disk is depicted with rays extended toward Akhenaton and his wife Nofretete. From the
tomb of Ramose.

mysterious in religion, Atonism spoke of the deity's nearness and
presence in the affairs of daily life. Atonism had no dark courts
or mysterious rites. Its ritual was quite simple, with hymns sung
by the temple choir and the presentation of gifts of meat and
drink by worshipers. The odors of perfume and the presence of
flowers added aesthetic qualities to the simple acts of worship.
On the occasion of royal visits, which must have been quite fre-
quent, the king personally consecrated the offerings.

Atonism never became the popular faith of Egypt, but it did
spread beyond the confines of Akhetaton. Memphis had an Aton
temple, and Aton reliefs have been found at Heliopolis. Modern
students of religion sometimes charge that the Aton faith was
devoid of ethical content, but this is an argument from silence.
All of its literary remains consist of devotional literature — hymns
extolling the glories of Aton and tomb inscriptions which de-
scribe the piety of his faithful worshipers. Whether or not Atonism was self consciously pacifist in orientation may be debated.
A universal faith minimizes the differences among men, and
Akhenaton's failure to intervene in the affairs of his Asiatic
subjects may indicate that he hoped that a peaceful policy would

resolve international tensions. Perhaps we should conclude that Akhenaton chose to devote himself to religious matters, and that the chaos in Asia was a result of neglect rather than self-conscious policy.

The Amarna tomb inscriptions give extravagant praise to Aton and his son, the Pharaoh:

> How prosperous is he who hears thy doctrine of life and is sated with beholding thee, and unceasingly his eyes look upon Aton every day.
>
> Thou art my great servant who hears my doctrine. My heart is content with every commission thou performest and I give thee the office in order that thou mayest eat the victuals of Pharaoh, the lord in the house of Aton.[3]

MOSES AND ATON

Since Akhenaton's worship of Aton as "sole god" is earlier than the date commonly ascribed to Moses (*ca.* 1280 B.C.), historians have puzzled over possible relationships between the monotheism of Akhenaton and the Biblical concept of one God. Sigmund Freud in his *Moses and Monotheism* sought to trace the Hebrew-Christian faith to the Amarna revolt of Akhenaton.

The principal reason for associating Moses with Atonism is the fact of his birth and education in Egypt. The Scriptures assert, however, that the religious impetus of Moses did not come from Egyptian sources, which he completely disavowed (cf. Exod. 18:10-11). It was in the wilderness that Moses had the religious experiences which prepared him to become the leader of the Exodus (Exod. 3:1-6). Jethro, Moses' Midianite father-in-law, worshiped Yahweh (Exod. 18:10-12) and Moses may have learned much from him. Yahwism and the religion of Egypt were completely and self-consciously opposed to one another. Israel firmly believed that Yahweh, their God, had defeated Pharaoh and the gods of Egypt in the experience of the Exodus.

THE DEATH OF ATON

Within a generation after the death of Akhenaton, Atonism was dead, and its leading exponent was contemptuously called, "that criminal of Akhetaton." The religion never had a popular base, and that disintegration of the empire might effectively be charged to the displeasure of Amon at his neglect. The government was moved back to Thebes, and Akhenaton's son-in-law, Tutankhaton ("the living image of Aton"), became Tutankh-

---

3 M. Sandman, *Texts for the Time of Akhenaton* 92. 8-9, 60.6; 1. 7-9, 80.17-81.1

amon ("the living image of Amon"). The cycle was now complete. Thebes and Amon had been restored to their former place of supremacy, the monuments erected by Akhenaton were defaced and the Aton temple was removed stone by stone. By the time of Moses, Akhetaton was abandoned completely, and Atonism had been forgotten.

Akhenaton Worshiping Aton. Akhenaton, his wife Nofretete, and one of their daughters stand with hands raised as they present offerings to Aton. Rays from the sun disk end in hands, two of which hold the Egyptian sign of life (ankh) before the faces of the Pharaoh and his queen.

V

THE HYMN TO THE ATON

Our most important source for knowledge of the Aton cult is found in the tombs of the nobles east of Akhetaton. These tombs include reliefs bearing hymns in praise to Aton and to his son, Akhenaton. Either the Pharaoh composed them himself, or they were composed by courtiers who had completely assimilated the religious convictions which were basic to his reforms. The so-called long hymn to Aton not only extols the glories of the god of Akhenaton, but it also contains expressions which have become a part of Egyptian, and even Hebrew devotional literature. The Long Hymn was inscribed on the walls of the tomb prepared for the priest and courtier Eye who had known Akhenaton from his youth.[1] James H. Breasted suggested that it was an excerpt from the ritual of the Aton temple.[2]

THE SPLENDOR AND POWER OF ATON

> Thou dawnest beautifully on the horizon of heaven,
> Oh living Aton, the beginner of life.
> When thou risest on the eastern horizon
> Thou fillest every land with thy beauty.
> Thou art beautiful, great, glittering, and high
>   over every land.
> Thy rays encompass the lands to the limit of all
>   that thou hast made.
> Thou art Re, and thou reachest to their end.[3]
> Thou subjectest them to thy beloved son.[4]

---

1 M. Sandman, *Texts from the Time of Akhenaton* pp. 93-96
2 *The Dawn of Conscience* (New York: 1933) pp. 286-87
3 The words "Re" (meaning "the sun") and "end" are similar in Egyptian. The principal shrine of Re was at Heliopolis.
4 The Pharaoh was regarded as the son of Aton, hence divine in his own right.

Though thou art far away, thy rays are on the earth;
Though thou art before men, no one sees
    thy movements.

NIGHTTIME

When thou settest in the western horizon
The earth is in darkness, like death.[5]
The night is passed in a bed-chamber with
    heads covered.
One eye sees not the other.
All their belongings which are under their heads
    might be stolen,
And they would not know it.
Every lion comes forth from his den,[6]
    and all snakes bite.
Darkness broods, the earth is still,
While he who made them rests in his horizon.

DAYTIME

At daybreak, when thou arisest on the horizon,
Shining as Aton by day,
Thou drivest away the darkness, and givest thy rays.
The Two Lands[7] are in festivity every day.
Men awaken and stand on their feet,
For thou hast lifted them up.
When they wash their bodies they put on
    their clothing,
And their arms are raised in praise at
    thy glorious appearing.
The entire land does its work.[8]
All cattle are content in their pastures;
The trees and plants flourish;
The birds fly from their nests,

---

5 Cf. Psalm 104:20, "Thou makest darkness and it is night when all the beasts of the forest creep forth."

6 Cf. Psalm 104:21, "The young lions roar for their prey, seeking their food from God."

7 The Two Lands are: Upper Egypt, the Nile Valley from the First Cataract to the head of the Delta; and Lower Egypt, the Delta region. The two Egypts were united ca. 3000 B.C. to form the united Egypt of subsequent history. Pharaohs continued to bear the title, "King of Upper and Lower Egypt" throughout ancient Egyptian history.

8 Cf. Psalm 104:22-23, "When the sun arises, they get them away and lie down in their dens. Man goes forth to his work, and to his labor until the evening."

Their wings are stretched out in praise
   to thy spirit.[9]
All beasts spring to their feet,
Whatever flies and alights;
They live when thou arisest for them.[10]
The ships are sailing upstream and downstream
For every road is open at thy appearing.
The fish in the river leap up before thee,
Thy rays are in the midst of the great green sea.[11]

THE CREATION: MAN

Who causest semen to grow in women,
Who makest water into mankind;
Who bringest to life the son in the womb
   of his mother;
Soothing him that he may not weep.
Thou nurse, even in the womb;
Who givest breath to sustain all that thou
      hast made.
And he comes forth from the womb on the day
   of his birth.
Thou openest his mouth completely;
Thou suppliest his necessities.

THE CREATION: ANIMAL LIFE

The chick in the egg chirps in the shell.
Thou givest him breath within it to make him live.
When thou hast made his time in the egg, to break it,
He comes forth from the egg to speak of
   his completion.
He walks upon his legs when he comes forth from it.

ATON'S GLORY IN CREATION

How manifold are thy works,
They are hidden from the face of man,
O sole god, like whom there is no other.

---

9 The spirit (Egyptian *ka*) was regarded as the vital principle or fundamental nature of a person. "In praise to thy *ka*," is, essentially, "In praise to thee."

10 Psalm 104:10-14, "Thou makest springs to gush forth in the valleys; they flow between the hills, they give drink to every beast of the field; the wild asses quench their thirst. By them the birds of the air have their habitation; they sing among the branches. From thy lofty abode thou waterest the mountains; the earth is satisfied with the fruit of thy work. Thou dost cause the grass to grow for the cattle, and plants for man to cultivate."

11 The "great green sea" is the Mediterranean. Cf. Psalm 104:25-26, "Yonder is the sea, great and wide, which teems with things innumerable, living things both small and great. There go the ships, and Leviathan which thou didst form to sport in it."

Thou didst create the world according to thy desire.
Whilst thou wast alone.[12]
Even all men, herds and flocks;
Whatever is on earth; creatures that walk
upon their feet;
And that soar aloft, flying with their wings.
The countries of Syria and Cush, the land of Egypt;
Thou settest every man in his place;
Thou suppliest their necessities.
Everyone has his food and his days are reckoned.[13]
Their tongues are diverse in speech,
And their characters likewise.
Their complexions are distinguished,
For thou distinguishest country from country.

ATON WATERS THE EARTH

Thou makest a Nile in the netherworld;
Thou bringest it forth at thy pleasure,
To give life to the people of Egypt.[14]
For thou madest them for thyself,
Thou lord of all who travailest with them;
Thou lord of every land who shinest for them;
The Aton of the day, great in majesty.
All distant lands; thou givest them life also,
For thou hast set a Nile in the sky.[15]
That it may descend for them and make waves
upon the mountains,[16]
Like the great green sea,
To water their fields in their villages.

ATON: LORD OF THE SEASONS

How efficacious are they plans, O lord of eternity.
There is a Nile in the sky for the foreign peoples,
But the (true) Nile comes from the nether-world
for the land of Egypt.
And for the animals of every country, that walk
upon their feet;

---

12 Cf. Psalm 104:24, "O Lord, how manifold are thy works, in wisdom hast thou made them all; the earth is full of thy creatures."
13 Cf. Psalm 104:27, "These all look to thee to give them their food in due season."
14 The Nile which watered Egypt was thought to have its source in a subterranean river which provided water for Egypt's Nile.
15 Egypt, essentially rainless, received its water from the Nile. Foreign lands, however, received water from rains, hence the reference to a "Nile in the sky."
16 Cf. Psalm 104:6, 10, "Thou didst cover it with the deep as with a garment: . . . Thou makest springs gush forth in the valleys, they flow between the hills."

Thy rays nourish every garden;
When thou shinest forth they live and
  they grow for thee.
Thou makest the seasons in order to prosper
  all thou hast made:
The winter to cool them, and the summer heat
  that they may taste thee.
Thou hast made the distant sky to shine in it,
And to see all that thou hast made.
Whilst thou wert alone,
Shining in thy form as the living Aton,
Appearing gloriously, and gleaming, being both
  distant and near.
Thou makest millions of forms through thyself alone,
Towns, villages, fields, roads, and rivers.
All eyes behold thee before them,
For thou art the Aton of the day over the earth.
Thou art in my heart,
And there is no other that knows thee,
Save thy son Nefer-Kheperu Re, Wa-en-Re.[17]
For thou hast made him wise in thy ways
  and in thy power.[18]

ATON'S PROVIDENCE

The earth came into being by thy hand,
  even as thou hast made them.
When thou dost shine, they live,
When thou settest, they die.
Thou, thyself, art length of life;
For men live only by thee.
Eyes are fixed on beauty until thou settest;
All work is laid aside when thou settest in the west,
But when thou risest again, everything is made
  to flourish for the king. . . .
Every leg is in motion, since thou didst establish
  the earth.
Thou raisest them up for thy son, who came forth
  from thy body.

The King of Upper and Lower Egypt, Lord of the Two Lands,

---

17 Names of Akhenaton
18 The Egyptian Pharaohs were both gods, and intermediaries between the gods and the people of Egypt.

Nefer-kheperu-Re, Wa-en-Re, son of Re, living in truth, lord of
Diadems, Akhenaton, whose life is long; and for the Chief Royal
Wife, Nefer-neferu-Aton, Nofertiti whom he loves, may she
live and flourish for ever and ever.

Although the Hymn to the Aton clearly grants a favored position to Egypt, Aton is pictured as holding sway over all peoples, for the sun brings light and heat to men of every nation.
This universalism finds a modern counterpart in the hymn of
Joseph Addison (1712):

> The spacious firmament on high,
> With all the blue ethereal sky,
> And spangled heavens, a shining frame,
> Their great Original proclaim:
> Th' unwearied sun, from day to day,
> Does his creator's power display,
> And publishes to every land
> The work of an almighty hand.

Parallels between the Hymn to the Aton and Psalm 104 suggest that the poetic expressions of the hymn became a part of the
literary heritage of the Near East. Although Atonism as a religion died a short time after the death of its chief apostle,
Akhenaton, poetic utterances used in praise to Aton could
readily be incorporated into other Egyptian devotional literature
and, eventually, find an echo in the literature of other lands.
While many of the similarities between Psalm 104 and Akhenaton's Hymn could arise from independent contemplation of the
movements of the sun on the part of people with no contact
whatever, the numerous contacts between Israel and Egypt at
least suggest that devotional language as well as proverbs (cf.
I Kings 4:30) were common knowledge among the two peoples.

The two compositions are basically different, however, in
that the Biblical psalmist acknowledges Yahweh, the God of
creation and providence, as a spiritual being associated with
natural phenomena only as their creator, whereas Aton, Akhenaton's "sole god" is identified with the disk of the sun. While
Akhenaton seems to have spiritualized the Egyptian sun worship, he never divorced himself completely from it. Biblical
monotheism asserts that the One God made "lights in the firma-
ment of heaven to give light upon the earth" (Gen. 1:15). The
Hymn of the Aton reaches a high point in the devotional
literature of Egypt, but its monotheism was radically different
from that presented on the pages of Scripture.

VI

THE AFFAIRS OF EMPIRE

The Amarna tablets enable us to see evidences of the decline of Egyptian power and prestige during the latter years of the reign of Amenhotep III and throughout the reign of Amenhotep IV (Akhenaton). About forty of them record correspondence between the rulers of Egypt and the rulers of the major powers of the Amarna Age. We find letters from the Kassite kings Kadashman-Enlil I and Burnaburiash II of Babylon, from Ashur-uballit I of Assyria, from Tushratta of Mitanni, from the Hittite king Suppiluliumas, and from an unnamed king of Alashia (Cyprus).

The Kings of Mitanni

In upper Mesopotamia, Egypt had an ally in Mitanni, a kingdom comprised largely of Hurrians (Biblical Horites), with an Indo-Aryan ruling class. The Mitannian kingdom was established about 1500 B.C. and at the height of its power reached from Nuzi and Arrapkha in Assyria to Alalakh in Syria. Its capital, Wassukkanni, was on the upper Habur River. A major threat both to Mitanni and, ultimately, to Egypt, came from the rising Hittite Empire with its capital at Hatusa (modern Bogazkoy) on the great bend of the Halys River in Asia Minor. Babylon had suffered an eclipse since the empire of Hammurabi and during the Amarna age it was ruled by a mountain people known as Kassites. Assyria, north of Babylon, had been subject to Mitanni until the Hittite conquest of Mitanni gave the Assyrians an opportunity to free themselves and develop an independent state.

The kings of Mitanni sent daughters to grace the harems of the Pharaohs of Egypt, and desired gold in exchange. The Amarna tablets include seven letters from Tushratta of Mitanni

to Amenhotep III, one to his widow Queen Tiy, and three to
Amenhotep IV (Akhenaton). In a typical communication he
writes to Amenhotep III:

> Let my brother send gold in very great quantity, without measure
> — that is what my brother should send me — and let my brother
> send more gold than (he sent) to my father, for in my brother's
> land gold is as plentiful as dust. May the gods so direct that,
> although now gold is so plentiful in my brother's land, he may
> have gold ten times more plentiful than now. Let not the gold
> which I desire trouble the heart of my brother, and let not my
> brother grieve my heart. So let my brother send me gold, without
> measure, in very great quantity.[1]

Although Tushratta's lust for gold may not have been appreciated in Thebes, Egypt valued her Mitannian allies who served as
a check on the ambitious Hittites, thereby helping Egypt main-
tain control over Syria and Palestine. Not only were princesses
from Mitanni welcome in Egypt, but the Mitannian gods might
be of help to the Egyptians. During the illness of Amenhotep
III, Tushratta sent a statue of the goddess Ishtar from Nineveh
to bless the ailing Pharaoh:

> Thus saith Ishtar, mistress of all the lands, "To Egypt, to the
> land which I love I will go; I will return." Verily I have now sent
> her, and she is gone. Indeed in the time of my father the
> mistress (Ishtar) went to that land, and inasmuch as she was re-
> vered when she formerly resided there, so now may my brother
> tenfold more than formerly honor her. May my brother honor
> her and joyfully send her back, and may she return. May Ishtar,
> mistress of heaven, protect my brother and me one hundred thou-
> sand years, and may our lady give to us both great joy.[2]

Tushratta looked to Egypt for help against Suppiluliumas
and the emerging Hittite Empire, but neither gold nor troops
came. Akhenaton was singing the praises of Aton in Akhetaton
when the Hittites succeeded in entering and sacking the Mitannian capital (ca. 1370 B.C.) and Tushratta was slain by one
of his own sons. The former king's exiled brother and rival,
Artatama, seems to have seized control in the confusion that
followed. Tushratta's son Mattiwaza (who may have been his
father's murderer) fled to the Hittites, and Shutarna, son of
Artatama, sought the friendship of the Assyrians in his bid for
the throne.

EMERGING ASSYRIA

The Mitannian Empire was at an end. Mattiwaza gained
Hittite support and took the throne of Mitanni with the aid of

---

1 Text 19, lines 59-67. The classification follows J. A. Knudtzon, *Die El-Amarna
Tafeln* (Leipzig: 1907-15)
2 Text 23, lines 13-29

Suppiluliumas' army. He remained a vassal of the Hittites, however, and his marriage to a daughter of Suppiluliumas further strengthened Hittite power in Mitanni. At the same time Ashuruballit of Assyria took advantage of the situation to seize the portion of Mitanni nearest to him. Assyria had been controlled alternately by Mitanni from the west and by Babylon from the south, but Ashuruballit determined to head an independent state.

To strengthen his position, Ashuruballit sent messengers to Akhenaton with a present of two white horses and a silver chariot. The letter accompanying these gifts[3] asks nothing in return, but a second letter[4] mentions a new palace that Ashuruballit is building, with the suggestion, "If thou art very friendly disposed, then send much gold."

Evidently the Assyrian embassy was received with courtesy in the court of Akhenaton, for Burnaburiash of Babylon was unhappy at the thought that Egypt would deal with a people who had been subject to Babylon. In anger he dispatched a letter:

> To Niphururia (i.e., Akhenaton), king of Egypt, say. Thus says Burnaburiash, king of Karduniash (i.e., Babylon), brother. I am well. May it be well with you, your house, your wives, your sons, your land, your chief men, your horses, your chariots. Since my fathers and your fathers established friendly relations with one another they sent rich presents to one another, and they refused not any good request one of the other. Now my brother has sent (only) two minas of gold as a present. But now, if gold is plentiful send me as much as your fathers, but if it is scarce send half of what your fathers did. Why did you send (only) two minas of gold. Now, since my work on the House of God is great, and I have undertaken its accomplishment vigorously, send much gold. And you, whatsover you desire from my land, write and it shall be brought to you. In the time of Kurigalzu, my father, the Canaanites as one man wrote to him saying, "We will go against the border of the land (i.e., Egypt), and we will stage an invasion, and we will make an alliance with you." But my father wrote to them saying, "Cease speaking of an alliance with me. If you are hostile against the king of Egypt, my brother, and ally yourself with another, I will come and will plunder you for he is in alliance with me." My father did not listen to them for the sake of your father. Now, concerning the Assyrians, my subjects, have I not written to you? If you love me you will not do business with them. Let them accomplish nothing. As a present I have sent to you three minas of beautiful lapis-lazuli, and five span of horses for five wooden chariots.[5]

---

3 Text 15
4 Text 16. The quotation is from lines 32 and 33
5 Text 9

THE HITTITE CHALLENGE

The Egyptians, however, did not give serious attention to their Asian Empire until the reigns of Seti I (1318-1299 B.C.) and Rameses II (1299-1232 B.C.). During the half century following the fall of Mitanni the Hittites met no serious opposition in their desire to control the whole of northern Mesopotamia and the Mediterranean coastal region of Syria. Not only was a daughter of Suppiluliumas married to the ruler of the vassal kingdom of Mitanni, but a son, Telepinus, was installed as ruler of Aleppo in Syria. The Amorites who had been vassals to Egypt were glad to welcome Hittite aid in establishing their independence. North Syria, or Amurru, became a hotbed of anti-Egyptian feeling, and Amorite princes served as unconscious pawns of Suppiluliumas in weakening Egyptian control in the area and preparing the way for Hittite domination.

Most of the Amarna letters were written by princes of city states in Syria, Phoenicia, and Canaan who asknowledged sovereignty but expressed the fear that rival princes or alien peoples might gain the upper hand. Some of the letters represent factional disputes among leaders both of whom protest their loyalty to Egypt. Among the rulers in Syria and Palestine we find letters from Akizzi of Qatna, Abdi-Ashirta and his son Aziru of Amurru (i.e., the Amorites), Rib-Addi of Byblos, Ammunira of Beirut, Zimrida of Sidon, Abimilki of Tyre, and Abdi-Khepa of Jerusalem. Other letters were sent from Hazor, Akko, Megiddo, Gezer, Ashelon, and Lachish. In some instances minor Egyptian officials wrote the letters.

RIB-ADDI OF BYBLOS

Rib-Addi of Byblos was threatened by Abdi-Ashirta and his son Aziru, Amorite rulers who followed the Hittite "party line" in seeking to remove northern Syria from the Egyptian sphere of influence. Gebal, or Gubla, was the ancient name of Byblos, a city which carried on commerce with Egypt as early as 3000 B.C. Excavations have produced a cylinder from the Thinite period of Egyptian history when the earliest Pharaohs occupied the throne. Vases discovered at Byblos bear the names of ancient Pharaohs including Mycerinus (twenty-seventh century B.C.), Unis and Pepi (twenty-fourth century B.C.). From the port of Byblos, Egypt imported cedars and spruce for use in building ships. Ships of Byblos also carried jars of oil, spices, wine, and leather.

Although Rib-Addi wished to continue to serve as a loyal vassal of Egypt, the chaos of the political situation pressed heavily upon him. The Amarna collection includes fifty-three letters which he addressed to Amenhotep II and Akhenaton warning them of the difficulty of the situation. In one of them he notes:

> Abdi-Ashirta has written to the warriors, "Assemble yourselves in the house of Ninib, and we will fall upon Byblos." . . . Thus have they formed a conspiracy with one another, and thus have I great fear that there is no man to rescue me out of their hand. Like birds that lie in a net, so am I in Byblos. Why do you hold yourself back in respect to your land? Behold, thus I have written to the palace, and you have paid no attention to my word. . . . What shall I do in my solitude? Behold, thus I ask day and night.[6]

Abdi-Ashirta and his son Aziru also wrote letters to Egypt affirming their loyalty. Two of them were addressed by Aziru to Dudu, an officer of the Egyptian court with a Semitic name. Evidently Dudu occupied a place in the court of Akhenaton comparable to that which Joseph occupied some years before (Gen. 41:37-57). Aziru wrote:

> To Dudu, my lord, my father.
> So says Aziru, your son your servant:
> At the feet of my father I will fall down. May my father be well. Dudu, behold I have performed the wish of the king, my lord, and whatever may be the wish of the king, my lord, let him write and I will perform it. Further: Behold, you are there, my father, and whatever is the wish of Dadu, my father, write, and I will indeed perform it. Behold you are my father and my lord, and I am your son. The lands of Amurru are your lands, and my house is your house, and all your wish, write, and indeed I will perform your wish. And indeed you are sitting before the king, my lord. Enemies have spoken slanderous words to my father before the king, my lord. But do not admit them. May you sit before the king, my lord, when I arise, and do not admit against me slanderous words. I am a servant of the king, my lord, and I will never depart from the words of the king, my lord, and from the words of Dudu my father. But if the king, my lord does not love me but hates me, what shall I then say?[7]

There can be no doubt that Rib-Addi, and not Aziru, was truly loyal to Egypt, for Aziru had made an alliance with Egypt's enemies, the Hittites. Writing to the Egyptian Pharaoh, Rib-Addi complained:

> I have written to the king, my lord: "They have taken all my cities. The son of Abdi-Ashirta is their lord. Byblos is the only

---

6 Text 74, lines 30-65
7 Text 158. The terms "father" and "son" are used to show respect. Aziru was the son of Abdi-Ashirta.

city that belongs to me." And have I not sent my messenger to the king, my lord? But you did not send soldiers, and you did not permit my messenger to leave. . . . Send him with auxiliaries. If the king hates his city, then I will abandon it, and if he permits me, an old man, to depart, then send your man that he may protect it. Why was nothing given me from the palace? I have heard of the Hati people (i.e. the Hittites) that they burn the lands with fire. I have repeatedly written but no answer has come to me. All lands of the king, my lord, are conquered, and my lord holds himself back from them, and behold, now they bring soldiers from the Hati lands to conquer Byblos. Therefore care for thy city.[8]

Rib-Addi stood alone in defending Byblos, but the force of the enemy proved too much. He fled to Beirut where he found refuge in the palace of its prince, Ammunira, with whom he was related by marriage. Byblos fell, but Rib-Addi still hoped for aid from Egypt to win it back. From Beirut he wrote:

If the king holds back in respect to the city, all the cities of Canaan (Kinahni) will be lost to him. . . . But let the king, my lord, quickly send archers that they may take the city at once.[9]

Finally Egypt did act. Aziru was apprehended and taken to Egypt where he was evidently detained for some time. A son of Aziru addressed a letter to the Egyptian official Dudu begging him for his father's release:

Aziru is your servant. Do not detain him there. Send him back quickly that he may protect the lands of the king, our Lord.

He goes on to mention "the Sudu people" who were taking advantage of Aziru's absence to further their own ends:

And all lands and all Sudu-people have said, "Aziru does not come from Egypt." And now the Sudu steal out of the lands and exalt themselves against me, saying, "Your father dwells in Egypt, so we will make hostility with you."[10]

We do not know what happened to Rib-Addi. By his own testimony he was an old man, but whether he died of natural causes or was a casualty in the battles of his generation we do not know. There seems to be a poetic justice in the fate of Aziru. As he had terrorized the Phoenician countryside, so his Amorite lands were terrorized by other tribes which were seeking a place for themselves in a time of general chaos. While Suppiluliumas backed Aziru, the Hittites were really only using him as a pawn to weaken Egyptian control in Asia and prepare the way for Hittite domination.

---

8 Text 126, lines 34-61
9 Text 137, lines 75-76; 97-99
10 Text 169, lines 12-15; 24-34

Lab'ayu of Shechem

The troublemaker in the region around Shechem was a man named Lab'ayu who, in league with the 'Apiru people, sought to control the central hill country of Canaan. Like Aziru, farther north, Lab'ayu sent letters to Egypt affirming his loyalty:

> Behold, I am a faithful servant of the king, and I have not committed a crime, and I have not sinned, and I do not refuse my tribute, and I do not refuse the demand of my deputy. Behold, I have been slandered and evil entreated but the king, my lord, has not made known to me my crime.[11]

Biridya of Megiddo, however, saw things differently:

> To the king, my lord and my sun, say: Thus says Biridya, the faithful servant of the king. At the feet of the king, my lord and my sun, seven and seven times I fall. Let the king know that ever since the archers returned, Lab'ayu has carried on hostilities against me, and we are not able to pluck the wool, and we are not able to go outside the gate in the presence of Lab'ayu since he has learned that you have not given archers, and now his face is set to take Megiddo, but let the king protect his city lest Lab'ayu seize it. Indeed, the city is destroyed by death from pestilence and disease. Let the king give one hundred garrison troops lest Lab'ayu seize it. Verily there is no other purpose in Lab'ayu. He seeks to destroy Megiddo.[12]

Biridya succeeded in capturing Lab'ayu, and plans were made to send him to Egypt. He was turned over to Zurata of Akko, an ally of Biridya, who was to send him to Egypt by ship. Zurata, however, accepted a bribe and released Lab'ayu.[13] His freedom was brief for Lab'ayu was murdered before he could reach home, but lawlessness continued as the sons of Lab'ayu continued to terrorize the countryside.[14]

Abdi-Khepa of Jerusalem

At least seven letters were addressed to the Pharaoh by Abdi-Khepa of Jerusalem, asking help in resisting the encroachments of a people known as 'Apiru. He notes:

> As sure as there is a ship in the midst of the sea, the mighty arm of the king conquers. Nahrim and Kapasi, but now the 'Apiru are taking the cities of the king. There is not a single governor remaining to the king, my lord. All have perished.[15]

Abdi-Khepa tends to classify all his enemies as 'Apiru, a word which in such contexts is practically synonymous with outlaw, or bandit. Things are so bad, Abdi-Khepa states, that the tribute

---

11 Text 254, lines 10-19
12 Text 244
13 Text 245
14 Text 246
15 Text 288, lines 33-40. Nahrim is the land of Mitanni; Kapasi may be Cush.

which he sent to Egypt was captured by these marauders on the plain of Ajalon.[16] This may have happened, but reports concerning Abdi-Khepa himself suggest that it would not have been beneath his dignity to concoct such a story to avoid paying tribute.

A neighboring king, Suwardata, thought to have been ruler of Hebron, complained:

> And the king, my lord, should know that Abdi-Khepa has taken my city out of my hand. Further, let the king, my lord, ask if I have taken a man, or even an ox or an ass from him. . . . Further, Lab'ayu who had taken our cities is dead, but verily Abdi-Khepa is another Lay'ayu and he takes our cities.[17]

On other occasions, however, Suwardata and Abdi-Khepa were allied against a common foe, the 'Apiru. Suwardata wrote:

> The king, my lord, should know that the 'Apiru have arisen in the land which the god of the king, my lord, has given me, and they have attacked it, and the king my lord, should know that all my brothers have abandoned me. I and Abdi-Khepa alone are left to fight against the 'Apiriu, and Zurata, the prince of Akko, and Indurata the prince of Achsaph, were the ones who hastened to my help.[18]

AMARNA AGE PALESTINE

The petty kings in Canaan were permitted their own armed forces comprising chariots, owned by the aristocracy, and footmen drawn from the peasant classes. Egypt did not interfere in local rivalries as long as her revenues continued to come and her commissioners were able to carry on the royal projects. When a local ruler had a grievance against his fellows, he could plead his case showing that the interests of Egypt would be best served by enabling him to defeat his rivals. This usually meant a request for troops — particularly bowmen. Egypt tolerated the perpetual squabbles of her subject states, and it may even have been a policy to allow such quarrels rather than to permit one state to gain enough power that it could forge an empire of its own.

Many of the strongholds held by the rulers of Canaanite city states had been fortified in Hyksos times. Egyptian control, however, was maintained through commissioners appointed by the Pharaoh to collect taxes and supervise the compulsory labor groups which worked on roads, tended the Lebanon forest preserves, or worked in the Valley of Esdraelon where wheat was

---

16 Text 287, lines 53-57
17 Text 280, lines 21-35
18 F. Turgeau-Dangin, "Nouvelles lettres d'el-Amarna," *Revue d'Assyriologie et d'Archeologie orientale,* XIX, pp. 91-108. Text 290a in S. A. B. Mercer, *The Tell el-Amarna Tablets* (Toronto: 1939)

grown for the royal court. Under strong Pharaohs, the interests of the Empire were carefully guarded, but the Amarna Age was a period during which Egyptian prestige was in eclipse and local rivalries became increasingly bitter. Only in extreme instances did Egypt interfere, and then it was usually too late to rectify matters.

A brief letter from Biridya of Megiddo indicates that forced labor (corvée) was expected of the subject states. Many, however, sensing the loss in Egyptian power failed to provide laborers for the royal projects:

> To the king, my lord and my sun, say: Thus Biridya, the true servant of the king, my lord and my sun, seven times and seven times I fall. Let the king be informed concerning his servant and concerning his city. Behold I am working in the town of Shunama, and I bring men of the corvée, but behold the governors who are with me do not as I do; they do not work in the town of Shunama; and they do not bring men for the corvée, but I alone bring men for the corvée from the town of Yapu. They come from Shunama and likewise from the town of Nuribda. So let the king be informed concerning his city.[19]

The 'Apiru

The identity of the 'Apiru (also written in cuneiform SA GAZ) has puzzled scholars since the discovery of the Amarna tablets. Some categorically affirmed that the 'Apiru are identical with the Biblical Hebrews, or Israelites, and that the Amarna tablets reflect the Canaanite version of events described in the Biblical book of Joshua.[20] Most scholars now agree that the 'Apiru cannot be identified with the Biblical Hebrews, although many suggest that the peoples are related. A strong argument against identification comes from the fact that 'Apiru appear in a wide variety of places of which there is no hint in the Biblical narrative. They appear in Sumer during the Ur III dynasty (ca. 2050 B.C.), in Larsa during the reigns of Warad-Sin and Rim-Sin (ca. 1770-1698B.C.), in Hammurabi's Babylon (ca. 1728-1686 B.C.), in Mari during the reign of Zimri Lim (ca 1730-1700 B.C.). They are mentioned in the large bodies of texts from Nuzi, Ugarit, and Bogazkoy. None of these references bear any relationship to the people of Israel.

In the Mari tablets the 'Apiru are described as a semi-nomadic people settled in the area between the Habur and the Balikh

19 F. Thureau-Dangin, op. cit., pp. 91-108: Mercer text 248a
20 This view was popularized by Sir Charles Marston in, The Bible Comes Alive (New York: n.d.), pp. 89-108. Marston felt that he could identify Joshua in the Amarna texts.

rivers, north of the Euphrates. The tablets from Alalakh mention that King Idrimi lived seven years among 'Apiru soldiers. Studies in the personal names of individuals designated 'Apiru in the Amarna and the Nuzi tablets have shown that they do not belong to any one ethnic group, although West Semitic names are most common in the Amarna texts.

There is considerable evidence that the 'Apiru were regarded as a social rather than an ethnic group. At Bogazkoy they are listed among the social classes and appear to have been classified between freemen and slaves. Wherever they appear they have one common trait — they are beyond the jurisdiction of the established authority. They frequently appear as a landless people who enter into dependent status as agricultural workers or soldiers in exchange for maintenance. The 'Apiru of the Amarna tablets are never described as invaders. They are people within the land who occupy areas not controlled by the larger towns. In a time of weak central government they sought to profit from the general confusion by challenging the city-states. Whatever their ethnic origins, they were doubtless joined by a variety of peoples from the oppressed elements of the population. To the rulers of Canaan, the 'Apiru were lawless bandits, a menace to society. Although 'Apiru is a much more inclusive term than Israel, the citizens of the city-states of Canaan probably thought of Joshua's army much as they regarded the 'Apiru of the Amarna Age.

Although the place names of the Amarna texts are parallel to those of the Old Testament, the personal names are totally different. In Joshua we read of Adoni-zedek, not Abdi-Khepa, as king of Jerusalem, and a number of other kings are named for the period of the conquest (cf. Josh. 10:3). Meredith G. Kline, who holds to the early date of the Exodus (1440 B.C.) has suggested that the conquest of Canaan by Joshua precedes the Amarna Age and that the 'Apiru of the Amarna letters may actually be the forces of Cushan Rishathaim, Israel's first oppressor during the time of the Judges. He concludes that the 'Apiru are not to be associated with Israel, but rather must be regarded as oppressors — the first of a series of such oppressors described in the Book of Judges.[21]

Most contemporary scholars date the conquest of Canaan after the Amarna Age, suggesting some time around 1280 B.C., as the

21 "The Ha-BI-ru — Kin or Foe of Israel?" *The Westminster Theological Journal* XIX-X), pp. 1-24; 170-184; 46-70

probable date of the Exodus.[22] This would place the Amarna Age in the period between Joseph and Moses. Aside from the fact that Israel was in Egypt during this time, and that they lost the favored position which they enjoyed in the days of Joseph, Scripture passes over this period with complete silence.

While we may not be able to pinpoint the exact chronology, the description of events in Canaan during the Amarna Age lends perspective to Biblical history during the years before the Monarchy. Local and tribal loyalties were more meaningful than imperial government, and centralized government was looked upon with suspicion (cf. Judg. 9:7-15).

---

22 So, for example, John Bright, *A History of Israel* (Philadelphia: 1959), p. 113; G. Ernest Wright, *Biblical Archaeology*, 2nd edition (Philadelphia: 1962), p. 60; Cyrus H. Gordon, *The World of the Old Testament* (Garden City: 1958), p. 144.

VII

TRADE AND COMMERCE DURING THE AMARNA AGE

By the Amarna Age the Mediterranean had become a highway for the ships of Egypt, Crete, Cyprus, Ugarit, the Phoenician cities, and even distant Mycenae. Land routes around the Fertile Crescent saw a steady stream of caravans bearing tribute to kings and items of trade for commoners. Horses and lapis lazuli were carried westward from Babylon, and its king Burnaburiash hoped for large quantities of Egyptian gold. Caravans were subject to attack, and Burnaburiash made it clear that it was the duty of Akhenaton to punish such offenders:

> Canaan (Kinahhi) is your land, and its kings are your servants. In your land I have been violently dealt with. Blind them (i.e., the raiders) and make good the money which they have stolen. Kill the people who murdered my servants and avenge their blood, for if you do not kill these people they will return, and my caravans, or even your messengers they will murder, and messengers between us will be intercepted, and if that happens, the inhabitants of the land will fall away from you.[1]

The king of Alashia (Cyprus) sent copper to Egypt, requesting silver and gold in exchange.[2] Iron, which in Hyksos times had twice the value of gold, became more plentiful during the Amarna Age. Tushratta of Mitanni sent iron to Egypt.[3] Iron, however, was not in common use in Israel until the time of David (I Chron. 22:3; 29:2). During the days of Saul, the Philistines had a monopoly on iron in Canaan:

> Now there was no smith to be found throughout all the land of Israel, for the Philistines said, "Lest the Hebrews make themselves swords or spears"; but every one of the Israelites went down to the Philistines to sharpen his plowshare, his mattock,

---

1 Text 8, lines 25-34
2 Text 34, lines 16-21; 35, lines 10-20
3 Text 22, column 1, line 38; column 2 lines 1, 3, 16

his axe or his sickle, and the charge was a pim for the plow-shares and for the mattocks, and a third of a shekel for sharpening the axes and setting the goads (I Sam. 13:19-21).

MINOAN CRETE

The great sea power of the eastern Mediterranean prior to the Amarna Age was Minoan Crete. The Cretans traded with Egypt from the earliest history of the two peoples. In addition to the direct route across the Mediterranean, the Minoans made use of an indirect trade route along the southwestern and southern shores of Asia Minor, and then southward by way of Cyprus to Egypt. The Egyptian word *Keftiu* (Hebrew *Caphtorim*, Gen. 10:14; Deut. 2:23; Amos 9:7) may be used of the peoples of southern Asia Minor as well as the inhabitants of Crete and its adjacent islands. The Philistines trace their ancestory to the *Caphtorim* (Amos 9:7), accounting for a non-Semitic element in southern Canaan.

Cretan trade with Egypt is depicted in the tomb of Rekhmire, lieutenant governor of Upper Egypt under Thothmes III (*ca.* 1490-1435 B.C.).[4] Here a prince of the *Keftiu* is depicted with gifts for the rulers of Egypt. Cretan power came to an abrupt end, however, some time around the end of the fifteenth century B.C., when Knossus, the capital, and other centers of Minoan culture were destroyed. The cause is not known, but Mycenaeans from mainland Greece may have been responsible, at least in part, for the fall of Knossus.

Early in the fourteenth century B.C., Mycenae became the cultural and political center of the Aegean world. Trade with Egypt brought to the Mycenaeans the ivory that appears frequently in their tombs. Scarabs discovered at Mycenae bear the names of Amenhotep III and his wife, Tiy.

THE PHOENICIANS

It was not the Mycenaeans, however, but the Phoenicians who succeeded the Minoans as the seafarers and the traders of the eastern Mediterranean. A tomb painting from Thebes shows Phoenician merchant ships tied up at docks along the Nile with their crews selling merchandise in the Egyptian bazaar. Amarna letters speak of Tyrian sailors and the wealth of their home port. Ships of Arvad also carry merchandise to Egypt. Phoenician control of the eastern Mediterranean was not challenged until

---

4 N. deG. Davies, *The Tomb of Rekh-mi-Re' at Thebes* (New York: 1943).

Rome fought a series of wars with Carthage, which began as a Phoenician colony. We know the conflicts as the Punic (ie., Phoenician) wars.

Commerce was not without its dangers. Roving bands of pirates from Lycia in Asia Minor infested the eastern Mediterranean and even landed on the coast of the Egyptian Delta. Amenhotep III found it necessary to organize a police force to patrol the Delta coast and keep the mouths of the Delta closed to all but lawful ships. The police manned customs houses and collected duty on all merchandise that was not consigned to the king. The land routes into Egypt were also policed, and admission was only granted to those with legitimate business.

VIII

THE ART OF AMARNA

Akhenaton's influence in art, like his religious beliefs, had antecedents and it would be improper to give him the credit — or blame — for all the art forms which found expression during the period of his reign. Nevertheless, under his inspiration we meet a new type of naturalism, almost an expressionism, coming to full flower. W. Stevenson Smith notes, "Men of ability . . . fell in with the ideas of Amenhotep IV and after a few tentative efforts, developed a new style with remarkable speed."[1] Bas reliefs show that Akhenaton was personally interested in art. He appears on visits to the sculptors' workshops in the company of Nofretete. Akhenaton's views of art are reflected in the royal monuments of his reign, the stelae that were erected to mark the boundaries of Akhetaton, and in the tombs prepared for government officials in the eastern desert.

SUNKEN RELIEF

One change in the Amarna Age art was purely mechanical. Sunken relief replaces the traditional raised relief in the ornamentation of the rock tombs. Davies comments on the technique:

> The rock in which they are hewn is far from having the uniform good quality which would invite bas-reliefs of the usual kind. Nor was Akhenaton willing, it appears, to employ the flat painting on plastered walls which was so much in vogue, and which the artists of Akhetaton also employed at times with good effect. The idea of modelling in plaster was conceived or adopted; and since figures in plaster-relief would have been liable to easy injury, the outline was sunk so far below the general surface as to bring the parts in highest relief just to its level. Nor was this the only measure taken to ensure durability. The whole design

---

1 *The Art and Architecture of Ancient Egypt* (Baltimore: 1958), p. 175

Amarna Style Head. A relief showing the characteristic art of the Amarna Age.

Queen Nofretete. The painted lime-stone bust shows the queen wearing a conical blue headdress encircled by a band to which the uraeus, symbol of royalty, is attached. The bust was found in the studio of the sculptor Thutmose at Akhetaton.

was first cut roughly in sunk-relief in the stone itself. Then a fine plaster was spread over it, covering all the inequalities and yet having the support of all points of a solid stone core. While the plaster was still soft, it was moulded with a blunt tool into the form and features which the artist desired. Finally the whole was painted, all the outlines being additionally marked out in red, frequently with such deviations as to leave the copyist in dilemma between the painted and the moulded lines.[2]

REALISM

Akhenaton's chief contribution to art, however, was anything but mechanical. Under his prodding, the artists at Akhetaton developed a realism — and even a distortion — which contrasts with the conservative, stylizing tendencies of earlier Egyptian art. The chief sculptor Bek describes himself on a stele as one "whom his majesty himself taught."

Arthur Weigall suggests that the innovations which Akhenaton brought into the art of his day were, in fact, a self-conscious return to earlier art forms. Young Akhenaton, Weigall assumes, would have discovered that the sun god Re-Harakhti was much more ancient than Amon of Thebes, and that ancient art forms differed from those in use during the Theban supremacy. In

---

2 *Op. cit.,* p. 18

reverting to the religious views of the Heliopolitan priesthood, Akhenaton would also have chosen to effect a renaissance of earlier art forms.[3]

Others have speculated on the possibility of Minoan influence on Akhenaton's art, noting that the Minoans adopted a naturalism which parallels that of Amarna, although Knossus was sacked some time during the reign of Amenhotep III. Barring the migration of Minoan artists to Akhetaton (which is rather unlikely), it may be best to see in the Amarna art forms a development based upon changes which were already being felt in art circles in Egypt. John A. Wilson notes that the older stylized art forms were on their way out as early as the reign of Thutmose III, and that the earlier tradition ended by the time of Hatshepsut.[4]

The naturalism of Akhenaton, however, goes far beyond his predecessors. The Pharaoh is not depicted in the splendid isolation of a god-king, but in the informal pose of a husband and father. Akhenaton habitually appears in the company of his wife, Nofretete, and their daughters, of whom ultimately there were six. A stele depicts Akhenaton kissing an infant while a second child sits on the queen's knee. Another shows a banquet scene with the king gnawing on a large piece of meat while his wife is eating roast fowl with her hands.

CARICATURE

Not only informality, but actual caricature tended to mark the art of Akhetaton. The natural deformities of the king were more than faithfully reproduced — they were exaggerated. The elongated skull, long thin neck, pointed chin, obtruding stomach, and abnormally large hips and thighs of the king may have been emphasized by artists who felt that any characteristic of a son of Aton deserves special attention.

The way in which people reacted to the king's wishes may be seen in a child's toy depicted at Akhetaton. A tomb painting "shows a model chariot drawn by monkeys. In the chariot is another monkey urging along his steeds (his receding forehead is terribly like the king's), by him a monkey princess prods the rump of the horse-monkeys which are jibbing and refusing to budge an inch in spite of a monkey groom who is dragging at their bridles for dear life."[5] Such caricature would indicate that

3 *Life and Times of Akhenaton* (London: 1922), p. 63
4 *The Burden of Egypt* (Chicago: 1954), p. 193
5 J. D. S. Pendlebury, *Tell el-Amarna* (London: 1935), p. 19

the "image" of Pharaoh as a son of Aton has been popularly
dispelled, and with it much of his power over his subjects.

TRANSITIONAL ART FORMS

The transition from the pre-Amarna art forms to those
encouraged by Akhenaton may be observed in the tomb of the
vizier Ramose in the Theban necropolis. Ramose first had a portrait of young Akhenaton carved in his tomb in the conventional
style, but later he added a second portrait in the new style. The
latter depicts Akhenaton standing with Nofretete beneath the
rays of the sun, bestowing golden necklets upon their faithful
vizier. Officials of the royal harem and a number of servants
look on. Akhenaton and his courtiers have the physical character-
istics which became conventional in Amarna art.

THE DEVELOPMENT OF AMARNA ART

The most violent break with the older convention came in the
early years of Akhenaton's reign. Before the move to Akhetaton,
the Theban hillside was dotted with tombs decorated with the
newer art forms and bearing inscriptions praising the Pharaoh.
With the move to Amarna, the art conventions matured. Artists
developed their own distinctive tastes and at times modified the
prevailing tendencies.

The painted stucco pavement which Petrie discovered in 1891
expresses the love of nature which the Aton cult encouraged. It
depicts a pool surrounded by clumps of flowers in which birds
are sporting and calves playing. Frescoes from the Green Room
of the North Palace, excavated by Francis Newton in 1924, represent the luxuriance of a papyrus thicket full of beautiful birds,
brightened up here and there by blue lotuses.

Some of the finest specimens of ancient Egyptian art have
come from the workshop of the sculptor Thutmose, discovered
by Ludwig Borchard during the German expedition at Amarna
prior to World War I. In preparing a series of heads of members
of the royal family, Thutmose chose to refine rather than to stress
their physical peculiarities. Thutmose based his work on keen
observation, augmented by casts taken from life when he wanted
to record the characteristic features of his subject. Among his
masterpieces are the famous painted limestone bust of Nofretete
— perhaps the best known piece of Egyptian art; and an un-
finished portrait of the queen now in the Cairo Museum.

IX

THE END OF AN ERA

The high hopes of Akhenaton's early years met an untimely end. The Asiatic provinces of Egypt fell away to the Hittites or to local Canaanite princes who had little sympathy with the Empire. Although there is no evidence of revolt in Egypt itself, Akhenaton's alienation from the older priesthood must have resulted in dislocations of the economy, and difficulties in the smooth running of government.

Smenkhkare

There is some evidence to suggest that Nofretete lost favor with her husband and moved to a new palace in the northern sector of Akhetaton. The king gave high honor to his eldest daughter Meritaton, whose husband, Smenkhkare became his successor on the throne of Egypt. We have no records indicating events in the earliest years of Smenkhkare's reign but in the third year he is known to have gone to Thebes. The reason for the visit can only be conjectured, but it may have been a gesture to appease the Amon priesthood which was still firmly entrenched there.

Our sources fail us again, but neither Akhenaton nor Smenkhkare are mentioned after *ca.* 1350 B.C. Whether they died natural deaths, or perished at the hands of assassins, can only be guessed. We are not even sure if Smenkhkare was co-regent with his father-in-law or if Akhenaton had died before he came to the throne. At most Smenkhkare reigned but four years. If his trip to Thebes was made to bring about a reconciliation with the Theban priesthood, it seems to have failed completely.

TUTANKHATON-TUTANKHAMON

Smenkhkare's successor, Tutankhaton, was married to Ankhes-enpaton, the third daughter of Akhenaton and Nofretete. Under Tutankhaton the capital was moved back to Thebes, and the Amarna revolt was at an end. His name, meaning "the living image of Aton," was changed to Tutankhamon, "the living image of Amon," and Amon was restored to his place as chief deity of Egypt. Ankhesenpaton's name was changed to Ankhes-enpamon for the same reason. Although Tuntankhamon was one of Egypt's lesser kings, the discovery of his tomb by Howard Carter in 1923 has made him the best known Pharaoh of Egyptian history to most westerners.

Tutankhamon's return to the worship of Amon was a conscious repudiation of the Aton cult. He actually ascribes the calamities that befell Egypt in the years of Akhenaton to the anger of Amon:

The Throne of Tutankhamon. The throne dates to the time before Tutankhamon renounced Atonism. His name appears as Tutankhaton in the inlay, but in the gold work where it could more easily be altered it has been changed to Tutankhamon. The back of the throne pictures the king and his wife under the sun disk (Aton).

Tutankhamon and His God. A black granite statue depicts the god Amon (large figure) with Pharaoh Tutankhamon, who renounced the Aton faith of Akhenaton and returned to Thebes, the center of the Amon priesthood.

The temples of the gods and goddesses . . . had gone to pieces. Their shrines had become desolate and had become overgrown mounds . . . The land was topsy turvy and the gods turned their backs upon this land. If one prayed to a god to seek counsel from him, he would never come (at all). If one made supplication to a goddess, similarly she would never come at all. Their hearts were hurt (?) so they destroyed that which had been made.[1]

Following Tutankhamon's early death we meet a story of intrigue and international politics which involves his widow. Ankhesenpamon, fearful of the future of herself and her country, wrote to the Hittite king, Suppiluliumas, asking that one of his sons be sent to Egypt to become her husband:

My husband died, and I have no son. People say that you have many sons. If you were to send me one of your sons, he might become my husband. I am loath to take a servant of mine and make him my husband.[2]

The Hittite king, suspecting something amiss, sent a servant to check on matters in Egypt. When the envoy reached Thebes, the widowed queen asked:

Why do you say, "They may try to deceive me." If I had a son would I write to a foreign country in a manner which is humiliating to myself and my country. You do not trust me and tell me such a thing. He who was my husband died and I have no sons. Shall I perhaps take one of my servants and make him my husband? I have not written to any other country. I have written only to you. People say that you have many sons. Give me one of your sons, and he is my husband and king in the land of Egypt.[3]

Suppiluliumas was convinced of the good faith of the young widow and sent a son to Egypt, but the young man never reached Thebes. Along the way he was murdered by Egyptians who resented the thought of a foreigner as their ruler. The result was a period of war between the Hittites and Egypt. Another son of Suppiluliumas made a record of the affair:

When my father gave them (the Egyptians) one of his sons (to take over the kingship), they killed him as they led him there. My father let his anger run away with him; he went to war against Egypt and attacked Egypt.[4]

The battle is not mentioned in the Egyptian annals. Probably it was brief and indecisive, for the Hittites could not afford to throw a major army into such a campaign. The rising power of Assyria was a threat to Hittite control in the north, and she had

1 J. Bennett, "The Restoration Inscription of Tut'Ankhamun," *Journal of Egyptian Archaeology*, XXV (1939), pp. 8-15
2 Albrecht Goetze, "Hittite Historical Texts," in *Ancient Near Eastern Texts*, James Pritchard, ed. (Princeton: 1955), p. 319
3 *Ibid.*
4 Albrecht Goetze, "Hittite Prayers," in *Ancient Near Eastern Texts*, James Pritchard, ed. (Princeton: 1955), p. 395

Horemhab. Granite statue of the commander of Tutankhaton's armies, later a Pharaoh in his own right.

to be ready to protect her northern provinces. Had the Hittites launched a major campaign against Egypt it is doubtful if she could have survived.

EYE AND HOREMHAB

The rule of Egypt fell to the aged vizier Eye, who had been a counselor and friend of Akhenaton. After four years Eye was succeeded by Horemhab (*ca.* 1340-1310 B.C.), an energetic ruler who sought to restore Egypt's fortunes abroad and erase the memory of the Amarna revolt at home. As a young general, Horemhab had espoused the cause of Akhenaton, but as a Pharaoh he sought to obliterate the records of the Amarna kings with as great enthusiasm as Akhenaton had sought to eliminate the name of Amon. Later orthodox king lists omit the names of Akhenaton, Smenkhkare, Tutankhamon, and Eye, placing the name of Horemhab immediately after Amenhotep III.

Although the Amon priests of Thebes seemed to be more firmly entrenched than ever after the accession of Horemhab, the calendar could not be pushed back completely. Egyptian art and literature retained some of the naturalism of the Amarna movement. There were effects in the religious world, too, for although Atonism was not pure monotheism, it exhibited tendencies in that direction which persisted in the Egyptian thought. God is frequently addressed in the singular, although under different names, in the hymns of the later periods of Egyptian history.

X

AMARNA AND THE BIBLE

The Amarna texts make it clear that the inhabitants of Canaan during the fourteenth and fifteenth centuries B.C. had a high degree of culture. While most people were probably illiterate, each community had its professional scribes who could write in at least one foreign language. Akkadian cuneiform, and not Canaanite, was the language of diplomatic correspondence between the city states of Canaan and the Egyptian court.

WRITTEN RECORDS

The Hebrew Scriptures give evidence that Israel made use of written records before the composition of the canonical Bible. References to the *Book of the Wars of the Lord,* and the *Book of Jasher,* appear in the Pentateuch and Joshua (Num. 21:14; Josh. 10:13). While the events which they commemorate may have first been passed on by word of mouth, the word "book" (*sepher,* inscription, written document) implies that they also were recorded in written documents. By the time of the Judges, a lad whom Gideon happened to meet along the road was able to write the names of twenty-seven men who were the elders of Succoth (Judg. 8:14).

The discovery of the Amarna Tablets created considerable interest in the matter of writing in ancient Canaan, and among the Israelites. Early in the twentieth century, Edouard Naville of the University of Geneva argued that the earliest documents of the Old Testament were written "in the idiom and with the characters of the Tel-el-Amarna tablets, namely Babylonian cuneiform," or Akkadian as we call it today.[1]

---

1 *Archaeology of the Old Testament: Was the Old Testament Written in Hebrew?* (London: 1913), p. 4

Naville went so far as to suggest that the Akkadian documents which lie behind our Hebrew Old Testament (or at least the Pentateuch and Joshua) were in use until the time of Ezra who adapted them to the alphabet used by the Aramaic speaking Jews of the Persian Empire. This view is not seriously considered today, for we know that Early or Palaeo-Hebrew manuscripts antedate the Square or Aramaic form of the letters in current use. The Canaanite dialect in use at Ras Shamra, ancient Ugarit, was written in a cuneiform alphabet at a time contemporary with the Amarna texts. Another group of texts, dated about 1500 B.C., was discovered at the Egyptian turquoise mines in the Sinai Peninsula. There are about twenty-five inscriptions in all, written in a form of alphabetic writing which was clearly derived from Egyptian hieroglyphics. Three short examples of the same alphabet, dating somewhat earlier than the Sinai inscriptions, have been discovered at Gezer, Lachish, and Shechem in southern Canaan. The oldest actual Hebrew inscription, using the Paleao-Hebrew script, is the Gezer Calendar (*ca.* 900 B.C.).

We cannot know for certain the nature of the writing on the tables, or tablets of the Law (Exod. 34:27-28). Moses, raised as an Egyptian prince, probably knew both Egyptian hieroglyphs and Akkadian cuneiform, and he may have learned to write in an early form of the Hebrew alphabet as a result of contacts with his own people. The Amarna texts have underscored the fact that both Egypt and Canaan were highly literate during the fifteenth and fourteenth centuries before Christ.

CANAANITE GLOSSES

Of particular interest to language students is the fact that the Amarna Letters frequently contain Canaanite words or expressions which are inserted to clarify the meaning of the Akkadian text, which was a foreign language to the scribe. These glosses are our earliest examples of the language which became Biblical Hebrew. While the language of Laban, and that branch of Abraham's family which settled in northern Mesopotamia, was Aramaic (cf. Gen. 31:47 where Laban uses an Aramaic name), the Patriarchs who entered Canaan came to speak "the language of Canaan" (cf. Isa. 19:18) which became the classical language of the Old Testament. The cuneiform syllabary in which the Amarna texts were written indicates vowel sounds which are not expressed in the alphabetic Hebrew script. In this way philologists are able to reconstruct some of the sounds of the ancient language.

AMARNA AGE PALESTINE

Although the Amarna texts do not name any personage met on the pages of Scripture, they are of value in helping us to visualize life in the Palestinian city states during the middle of the second millenium B.C. Biblical cities mentioned in the correspondence include: Akko, Ashkelon, Arvad, Aroer, Ashtaroth, Gebal (Byblos), Gezer, Gath, Gaza, Jerusalem, Joppa, Keilah, Lachish, Megiddo, Sidon, Tyre, Sharon, Shechem, Taanach, and Zorah. Beth-ninurta is thought to be identical with Biblical Beth-shemesh.

These cities are, for the most part, independent city states, owing allegiance to Egypt yet free to form their own alliances and resolve their own local problems. It was this type of political structure that Joshua met in Canaan. He waged war against "thirty-one kings" (Josh. 12:24). At times these kings made alliances in order to prevent Israel from gaining control of the land, just as the Amarna Age rulers aided one another in resisting Lab'ayu. A leader against Joshua was Adonizedek, king of Jerusalem, who found allies in Hoham, king of Hebron; Piram, king of Jarmuth; Japhia, king of Lachish; and Debir, king of Eglon (Josh. 10:1-3).

The military engagements were strictly limited affairs, judged by the numbers of troops and horses requested of the Pharaoh. Rib-Addi of Byblos pleaded:

> Let it seem good to the lord, the sun of the lands, to give me twenty pairs of horses.[2]

In his encounter with Abdi-Ashirta, the Amorite chieftan who was seeking to control northern Syria in league with the Hittites, Rib-Addi asked for but three hundred men.[3]

Abi-milki of Tyre indicated that he could get by with but token help from Egypt. In one letter he asks for but twenty foot soldiers,[4] and in another he will be satisfied with but ten.[5] Somewhat earlier, in the Canaan of Abraham's day, the patriarch was able to assemble an army of three hundred and eighteen men (Gen. 14:14), pursue a confederation of five kings with their armies, rout and chase the enemy. An entire garrison

---

2 Text 103, lines 39-43
3 Text 93, lines 10-12
4 Text 149, lines 17-19
5 Text 148, lines 13-17

might number but fifty men in the armies of Amarna Age rulers.[6]

AFFAIRS OF GOVERNMENT

The presence of a friend at the court was appreciated and cultivated by the rulers of the city states. Several of the Amarna tablets are addressed to an Egyptian official named Yanhumu who bore the title "the king's fanbearer." He was evidently a man of considerable power, for the king entrusted him with the issuing of supplies from a place known as Yarimuta. For this reason the local princes in Syria and Canaan frequently wrote to him. After outlining his needs, Rib-Addi indulged in a little apple-polishing as he concluded, "There is no servant like Yanhamu, a faithful servant of the king."[7]

Yanhamu seems to have occupied in the court of Amenhotep III (and possible Akhenaton as well) a position comparable to the one Joseph held several generations earlier.[8] Both Yanhamu and Joseph were charged with overseeing the distribution of food supplies (cf. Gen. 42:51-57). They both had Semitic names, and the presence of Yanhamu in an Egyptian court during New Kingdom times indicates that Semites were not barred from government following the Hyksos expulsion. Rulers often find it safer to trust faithful foreigners than some of their own subjects who might be tempted to rebel.

The simple tastes of the Israelite tribes in the period before the monarchy may be contrasted with the ostentation of Solomon's harem with its thousand wives and concubines (I Kings 11:3) along with the wealth and luxury of an oriental court. The rulers of the larger states of the Amarna Age, and particularly Tushratta of Mitanni, sent their daughters to grace the harems of Amenhotep III and Akhenaton. A scarab of Amenhotep III commemorates the arrival of Giluhepa, a Mitannian princess with a retinue of three hundred seventeen maidens.[9] That Amenhotep III was actively building his harem is shown in a letter which he addressed to Milk-ili of Gezer which says, in part:

> I have sent Hania, the commander of the archers, to you with all sorts of things, to bring the beautiful women. . . . There are in all

---

6 Text 238, lines 9-12
7 Text 118, lines 55-56
8 Problems of chronology are acute. H. H. Rowley, *From Joseph to Joshua* (London: 1950) argues that Joseph was actually Akhenaton's Prime Minister. Cf. pp. 119-120. Most contemporary scholars place Joseph's entry into Egypt in Hyksos times (ca. 1720-1550 B.C.). Cf. G. Ernest Wright, *Biblical Archaeology* (Philadelphia: 1962), pp. 53-58
9 The Scarab is reproduced in A. deBuck, *Egyptian Reading Book I* (Leiden: 1948), p. 67

forty women; forty pieces of silver is the price of the women. Send me therefore very beautiful women among whom are no slanderers, so that the king, your lord, may say to you, "This is fine."[10]

The building of a harem had political implications for it involved an alliance of friendship. Early in Solomon's reign he "made a marriage alliance with Pharaoh, king of Egypt; he took Pharaoh's daughter and brought her into the City of David. . . ." (I Kings 3:1). A large harem, moreover, was a symbol of power, wealth and prestige. Solomon was but adapting the customs of the great rulers of the ancient East when he built an enormous harem for himself.

10 Musees Royaux (Bruxelles) tablet E6753, edited by Georges Dossin in *Revue d'Assyriologie et d'Archaeologie orientale,* XXXI, pp. 125-136. Mercer Number 31a

BIBLIOGRAPHY

ARCHAEOLOGY

Budge, E. A. W., *By Nile and Tigris,* I (London: 1920), pp. 133-144

Pendelbury, J. D. S., *Tell el-Amarna* (London; 1935)

Peet, Thomas Eric; Woolley Leonard; Frankfort, Henri; Pendelbury, J. D. S., *et al. The City of Akhenaten* (Parts I-III), 4 volumes (London; 1923-51)

HISTORY

Aldred, C., "The End of the El 'Amarna Period," *Journal of Egyptian Archaeology* XLIII (1957), pp. 30-41

Baikie, James, *The Amarna Age* (New York: 1926)

Bratton, Fred Gladstone, *The First Heretic: The Life and Times of Ikhnaton the King* (Boston: 1961)

Gardiner, A. H., "The So-called Tomb of Queen Tiye," *Journal of Egyptian Archaeology,* XLIII (1957), pp. 10-25

Meyer, Eduard, *Geschichte des Altertums,* II (Stuttgart: 1955), pp. 303-426

Seele, K. C., "King Ay and the Close of the Amarna Age,"*Journal of Near Eastern Studies,* XIV (1955), pp. 168-180

Weigall, Arthur, *The Life and Times of Akhnaton* (London: 1923)

ART AND TOMB INSCRIPTIONS

Davies, N. deGaris, *The Rock Tombs of El Amarna* (Archaeological Survey of Egypt), 6 volumes (London: 1903-08)

Frankfort, Henri, ed. *The Mural Paintings of El 'Amarneh* (London: 1929)

Sandman, M. *Texts from the Time of Akhenaton* (Brussels: 1938)

Religion

Anthes, R., "Die Maat des Echnaton von Amarna," *Journal of the American Oriental Society*, Supplement 14 (1952)

The Amarna Tablets

Texts

Betzold, C., and Budge, E. A. W., *The Tell El Amarna Tablets in the British Museum* (London: 1892)

Winckler, H. and Abel, L., *Der Thontafelfund von El Amarna* (Berlin: 1889-90)

Transcription and Translation

Albright, W. F. and Mendenhall, George, "Akkadian Letters," in Pritchard, J. B., ed., *Ancient Near Eastern Texts* (2nd edition) (Princeton: 1955), pp. 482-490

Gordon, C. H., "The New Amarna Tablets," *Orientalia* XVI (1947), pp. 1-21

Knudtzon, J. A., *Die El-Amarna Tafeln* (with commentary by O. Webber and glossary by E. Ebeling (Leipzig: 1907-15)

Mercer, S. A. B., *The Tell el-Amarna Tablets* (Toronto: 1939)

Schroeder, O., *Die Tontafeln von El-Amarna* (Berlin texts only), (Leipzig: 1915)

Thureau-Dangin, F., "Nouvilles lettres d'el-Amarna," *Revue d'Assyriologie et d'archeologie orientale*, XIX (1922), pp. 91-108

Studies

Albright, W. F., "Cuneiform Material for Egyptian Prosopography, 1500-1200 B.C." *Journal of Near Eastern Studies*, V (1946), pp. 9-25

"The Egyptian Correspondence of Abimilki, Prince of Tyre," *Journal of Egyptian Archaeology*, XXIII (1937) pp. 190-203

"The Letters of 'Abdu-Kheba, Prince of Jerusalem," *Bulletin of the American Schools of Oriental Research*, Supplementary Studies, 1950

Campbell, Jr., Edward F., "The Amarna Letters and the Amarna Period," *Biblical Archaeologist*, XXIII (1960), pp. 2-22.

Van der Meer, P. "The Chronological Determination of the Mesopotamian Letters in the El Amarna Archives," *Ex Oriente Lux*, Jaarbericht No. 15, pp. 75-84

INDEX